THE HAREM WITHIN

Also by Fatima Mernissi

Islam and Democracy: Fear of the Modern World
The Forgotten Queen of Islam
Doing Daily Battle
Beyond the Veil: Male/Female Dynamics in
Modern Muslim Society
Women and Islam: An Historical and Theological Enquiry

THE
Harem
WITHIN

FATIMA MERNISSI

Doubleday

LONDON · NEW YORK · TORONTO · SYDNEY · AUCKLAND

TRANSWORLD PUBLISHERS LTD
61-63 Uxbridge Road, London W5 5SA

TRANSWORLD PUBLISHERS (AUSTRALIA) PTY LTD
15-25 Helles Avenue, Moorebank, NSW 2170

TRANSWORLD PUBLISHERS (NZ) LTD
3 William Pickering Drive, Albany, Auckland

Published 1994 by Doubleday
a division of Transworld Publishers Ltd
Copyright © Fatima Mernissi 1994

Photographs copyright © Ruth V. Ward 1994

A catalogue record for this book is
available from the British Library.
ISBN 0385 405421

Typeset in 11/15pt Bembo by
Falcon Graphic Art Ltd,
Wallington, Surrey
Printed in Great Britain by
Mackays of Chatham plc, Chatham, Kent.

Contents

1 *My Harem Frontiers* 1

2 *Scheherazade, the King, and the Words* 13

3 *The French Harem* 21

4 *Yasmina's First Co-Wife* 29

5 *Chama and the Caliph* 41

6 *Tamou's Horse* 51

7 *The Harem Within* 61

8 *Aquatic Dishwashing* 71

9 *Moonlit Nights of Laughter* 79

10 *The Men's Salon* 87

11 *World War II: View from the Courtyard* 99

12 *Asmahan, the Singing Princess* 109

13 *The Harem Goes to the Movies* 119

14 *Egyptian Feminists Visit the Terrace* 131

15 *Princess Budur's Fate* 143

16 *The Forbidden Terrace* 153

17 *Mina, the Rootless* 167

18 *American Cigarettes* 185

19 *Mustaches and Breasts* 199

20 *The Silent Dream of Wings and Flights* 213

21 *Skin Politics: Eggs, Dates, and Other Beauty Secrets* 231

22 *Henna, Clay, and Men's Stares* 243

THE HAREM WITHIN

1

My Harem Frontiers

I was born in a harem in 1940 in Fez, a ninth-century Moroccan city some five thousand kilometers west of Mecca, and one thousand kilometers south of Madrid, one of the dangerous capitals of the Christians. The problems with the Christians start, said Father, as with women, when the *hudud*, or sacred frontier, is not respected. I was born in the midst of chaos, since neither Christians nor women accepted the frontiers. Right on our threshold, you could see women of the harem contesting and fighting with Ahmed the doorkeeper as the foreign armies from the North kept arriving all over the city. In fact, foreigners were standing right at the end of our street, which lay just between the old city and the Ville Nouvelle, a new city that they were building for themselves. When Allah created the earth, said Father, he separated men from women, and put a sea between Muslims and Christians for a reason. Harmony exists when each group respects the prescribed limits of the other; trespassing leads only to sorrow and unhappiness. But women dreamed of trespassing all the time. The world beyond the gate was their obsession. They fantasized all day long about parading in unfamiliar streets, while the Christians kept crossing the sea, bringing death and chaos.

Trouble and cold winds come from the North, and we turn to the East to pray. Mecca is far. Your prayers might reach it if you know how to concentrate. I was to be taught how to concentrate when the time was appropriate. Madrid's soldiers had camped north of Fez, and even Uncle ꞔAli and Father, who were so powerful in the city and ordered around everyone in the house, had to ask permission from Madrid to attend Moulay Abdesslam's religious festival near Tangier, three hundred kilometers away. But the soldiers who stood outside our door were French, and of another tribe. They were Christians like the Spaniards, but they spoke another language and lived farther north. Paris was their capital. Cousin Samir said that Paris was probably two thousand kilometers away, twice as far away from us as Madrid, and twice as ferocious. Christians, just like Muslims, fight each other all the time, and the Spanish and the French almost killed one another when they crossed our frontier. Then, when neither was able to exterminate the other, they decided to cut Morocco in half. They put soldiers near 'Arbaoua and said from now on, to go north, you needed a pass because you were crossing into Spanish Morocco. To go south, you needed another pass, because you were crossing into French Morocco. If you did not go along with what they said, you got stuck at ꞔArbaoua, an arbitrary spot where they had built a huge gate and said that it was a frontier. But Morocco, said Father, had existed undivided for centuries, even before Islam came along fourteen hundred years ago. No one ever had heard of a frontier splitting the land in two before. The frontier was an invisible line in the mind of warriors.

Cousin Samir, who sometimes accompanied Uncle and Father

on their trips, said that to create a frontier, all you need is soldiers to force others to believe in it. In the landscape itself, nothing changes. The frontier is in the mind of the powerful. I could not go and see this for myself because Uncle and Father said that a girl does not travel. Travel is dangerous and women can't defend themselves. Aunt Habiba, who had been cast off and sent away suddenly for no reason by a husband she loved dearly, said that Allah had sent the Northern armies to Morocco to punish the men for violating the *hudud* protecting women. When you hurt a woman, you are violating Allah's sacred frontier. It is unlawful to hurt the weak. She cried for years.

Education is to know the *hudud*, the sacred frontiers, said Lalla Tam, the headmistress at the Koranic school where I was sent at age three to join my ten cousins. My teacher had a long, menacing whip, and I totally agreed with her about everything: the frontier, the Christians, education. To be a Muslim was to respect the *hudud*. And for a child, to respect the *hudud* was to obey. I wanted badly to please Lalla Tam, but once out of her earshot, I asked Cousin Malika, who was two years older than I, if she could show me where the *hudud* actually was located. She answered that all she knew for sure was that everything would work out fine if I obeyed the teacher. The *hudud* was whatever the teacher forbade. My cousin's words helped me relax and start enjoying school.

But since then, looking for the frontier has become my life's occupation. Anxiety eats at me whenever I cannot situate the geometric line organizing my powerlessness.

My childhood was happy because the frontiers were crystal clear. The first frontier was the threshold separating our family's salon from the main courtyard. I was not allowed to step out into that courtyard in the morning until Mother woke up, which meant that I had to amuse myself from 6 A.M. to 8 A.M. without making any noise. I could sit on the cold white marble threshold if I wanted to, but I had to refrain from joining in with my older cousins already at play. 'You don't know how to defend yourself yet,' Mother would say. 'Even playing is a kind of war.' I was afraid of war, so I would put my little cushion down on our threshold, and play *l-msaria b-lglass* (literally, 'The Seated Promenade'), a game I invented then and still find quite useful today. You need only three things to play. The first is to be stuck somewhere, the second is to have a place to sit, and the third is to be in a humble state of mind, so you can accept that your time is worth nothing. The game consists of contemplating familiar grounds as if they were alien to you.

I would sit on our threshold and look at our house as if I had never seen it before. First, there was the square and rigid courtyard, where symmetry ruled everything. Even the white marble fountain, forever bubbling in the courtyard center, seemed controlled and tamed. The fountain had a thin blue-and-white faience frieze all around its circumference, which reproduced the design inlaid between the square marble tiles of the floor. The courtyard was surrounded by an arched colonnade, supported by four columns on each side. The columns had marble at the top and the bottom, and blue-and-white tilework in the middle, mirroring the pattern of the fountain and floor. Then, facing one another in pairs, across the courtyard, were four huge salons. Each salon had a gigantic gate in the middle, flanked by enormous windows, opening onto the courtyard. In the early morning, and in the winter, the salon gates would be shut tight with cedarwood doors carved with flowers. In the summer, the doors would be opened and drapes of heavy brocade, velvet, and lace let down, so breezes could flow in while light and noise were kept away. The salon windows had carved wooden shutters on the inside, similar to the doors, but from the outside all you could see were silver-plated, wrought-iron grilles, topped with wonderfully colored glass arches. I loved those colored glass arches, because of the way the rising morning sun kept changing their reds and blues to different hues, and softening the yellows. Like the heavy wooden doors, the windows were left wide open in the summer and the drapes were let down only at night or during afternoon naptimes, to protect sleep.

When you lifted your eyes toward the sky, you could see an elegant two-story structure with the top floors repeating the square arched colonnade of the courtyard, completed with a parapet of silver-plated ironwork. And finally, you had the sky – hanging up above but still strictly square-shaped, like all the rest, and solidly framed in a wooden frieze of fading gold-and-ocher geometric design.

Looking at the sky from the courtyard was an overwhelming experience. At first, it looked tame because of the man-made square frame. But then the movement of the early morning stars, fading slowly in the deep blue and white, became so intense that it could make you dizzy. In fact, on some days, especially during winter, when the purple and shocking-pink rays of the sun violently chased the last, stubborn twinkling stars from the sky, you could easily have become hypnotized. With your head tilted back, facing the squared sky, you would feel like going to sleep, but just then people would start invading the courtyard, coming up from everywhere, the doors and the stairs – oh, I almost forgot the stairs. Lodged in the four corners of the courtyard, they were important because even grownups could play a sort of gigantic hide-and-go-seek on them, running up and down their glazed green steps.

Facing me across the courtyard was the salon of Uncle and his wife and their seven children, which was an exact reproduction of our own. Mother would not allow any publicly visible distinctions to be made between our salon and Uncle's, although Uncle was the firstborn son, and therefore traditionally entitled to larger and more elaborate living quarters. Not only was Uncle older and richer than Father, but he also had a larger immediate family. With my sister and brother and my parents, we only numbered five. Uncle's family totalled nine (or ten, counting his wife's sister who visited often from Rabat, and sometimes stayed as long as six months at a time, after her husband married a second wife). But Mother, who hated communal harem life and dreamt of an eternal tête-à-tête with Father, only accepted what she called the ᵓazma (crisis) arrangement on the condition that no distinction be made between the wives. She would enjoy the exact same privileges as Uncle's wife, despite their disparities in rank. Uncle scrupulously respected this arrangement because in a well-managed harem, the more power you have, the more generous you ought to be. He and his children ultimately did have more space, but it was on the top floors only, well away from the highly public courtyard. Power need not manifest itself blatantly.

Our paternal grandmother, Lalla Mani, occupied the salon to my left. We only went there twice a day, once in the morning to kiss her hand, and a second time in the evening to do the same. Like all the other salons, hers was furnished with silk brocade-covered sofas and cushions running along all four walls; a huge central mirror reflecting the inside of the gate door and its carefully studied draperies; and a pale, flowered carpet which completely covered the floor. We were never, never supposed to step on her carpet wearing our slippers – or even worse, with wet feet, which was almost impossible to avoid doing in the summer, when the courtyard floor was cooled twice a day with water from the fountain. The young women of the family, such as my cousin Chama and her sisters, liked to clean the courtyard floor by playing *la piscine* (swimming pool), that is, by throwing buckets of water onto the floor and 'accidently' splashing the person next to them. This, of course, encouraged the younger children – specifically, my cousin Samir and I – to run to the kitchen and come back armed with the waterhose. Then we would do a really good splashing job, and everyone would be screaming and trying to stop us. Our shouts would inevitably disturb Lalla Mani, who would angrily raise her drapes and warn us that she was going to complain to Uncle and Father that very night. 'I will tell them that no one respects authority in this house anymore,' she would say. Lalla Mani hated water splashing and she hated wet feet. In fact, if we ran to talk to her after we had been standing near the fountain, she would always order us to stop where we were. 'Don't talk to me with wet feet,' she would say. 'Go dry yourself first.' As far as she was concerned, anyone who violated the Clean-and-Dry-Feet Rule was stigmatized for life, and if we dared to go so far as to trespass on or dirty her flowered carpet, we were reminded of our wayward deed for many years to come. Lalla Mani appreciated being respected, that is to say, being left alone to sit elegantly dressed in her bejeweled headdress, and look silently out into the courtyard. She liked being surrounded by heavy silence. Silence was the luxurious privilege of the happy few who could afford to keep the children away.

Finally, on the right side of the courtyard was the largest and most elegant salon of all – the men's dining room, where they ate, listened to the news, settled business deals, and played cards. The men were the only ones in the house supposed to have access to a huge cabinet radio which they kept in the right corner of their salon, with the cabinet doors locked when the radio was not in use. (Loudspeakers were installed outside, however, to allow everyone to listen to it.) Father was sure that he and Uncle had the only two keys to the radio. However, curiously enough, the women managed to listen to Radio Cairo regularly, when the men were out. Chama and Mother often would be dancing away to its tunes, singing along with the Lebanese princess Asmahan

'*Ahwa*' (I am in love), with no men in sight. And I remember quite clearly the first time the grownups used the word *khain* (traitors) to describe Samir and myself: when we told Father, who had asked us what we had done while he was away, that we had listened to Radio Cairo. Our answer indicated that there was an unlawful key going around. More specifically, it indicated that the women had stolen the key and made a copy of it. 'If they made a copy of the radio key, soon they'll make one to open the gate,' growled Father. A huge dispute ensued, with the women being interviewed in the men's salon one at a time. But after two days of inquiry, it turned out that the radio key must have fallen from the sky. No one knew where it had come from.

Even so, following the inquiry, the women took their revenge on us children. They said that we were traitors, and ought to be excluded from their games. That was a horrifying prospect, and so we defended ourselves by explaining that all we had done was tell the truth. Mother retorted by saying that some things were true, indeed, but you still could not say them: you had to keep them secret. And then she added that what you say and what you keep secret has nothing to do with truth and lies. We begged her to explain to us how to tell the difference, but she did not come up with a helpful answer. 'You have to judge by yourselves the impact of your words,' she said. 'If what you say could hurt someone, then you keep quiet.' Well, that advice did not help us at all. Poor Samir hated being called a traitor. He rebelled and shouted that he was free to say whatever he wanted. I, as usual, admired his audacity, but kept silent. I decided that if, on top of trying to distinguish truth from lies (which was already giving me a lot of trouble), I also had to distinguish this new category of 'secret', I was headed for a lot of confusion, and I would just have to accept the fact that I often would be insulted and called a traitor.

One of my weekly pleasures was to admire Samir as he staged

his mutinies against the grownups, and I felt that if I only kept following him, nothing bad could happen to me. Samir and I were born the same day, in a long Ramadan afternoon, with hardly one hour's difference.[1] He came first, born on the second floor, the seventh child of his mother. I was born one hour later in our salon downstairs, my parents' first-born, and although Mother was exhausted, she insisted that my aunts and relatives hold the same celebration rituals for me as for Samir. She had always rejected male superiority as nonsense and totally anti-Muslim – 'Allah made us all equal,' she would say. The house, she later recalled, vibrated for a second time that afternoon, with the traditional *you-you-you-you*[2] and festive chants, and the neighbors got confused and thought that two baby boys had been born. Father was thrilled: I was very plump with a round face 'like a moon', and he immediately decided that I was going to be a great beauty. To tease him a little, Lalla Mani told him that I was a bit too pale, and my eyes were too slanted, and my cheekbones too high, while Samir, she said, had 'a beautiful golden tan and the largest black velvet eyes you ever saw.' Mother told me later that she kept quiet, but as soon as she could stand on her feet, she rushed to see if Samir really had velvet eyes, and he did. He still does, but all the velvety softness disappears when he is in his seditious moods, and I have always wondered whether his inclination to jump up and down when rebelling against the grownups was not merely due to his wiry build.

[1] Ramadan, the sacred ninth month of the Muslim calendar, is observed by daily fasting from sunrise to sunset.

[2] *You-you-you-you* is a joyous song women chant to celebrate happy events from birth and marriage to simple ones such as finishing an embroidery piece, or organizing a party for an old aunt.

In contrast, I was so plump then that it never occurred to me to leap when someone annoyed me; I just cried and ran to hide in my mother's caftan. But Mother kept saying that I could not rely on Samir to do all the rebelling for me: 'You have to learn to scream and protest, just the way you learned to walk and talk. Crying when you are insulted is like asking for more.' She was so worried that I would grow up to be an obsequious woman that she consulted Grandmother Yasmina, known to be incomparable at staging confrontations, when visiting her on summer vacations. Grandmother advised her to stop comparing me with Samir, and to push me instead to develop a protective attitude toward the younger children. 'There are many ways to create a strong personality,' she said. 'One of them is to develop the capacity to feel responsible for others. Simply being aggressive, and jumping at your neighbor's throat whenever he or she makes a blunder is one way, and surely not the most elegant one. Pushing a child to feel responsible for the younger ones in the courtyard gives her room to build strength. Hanging on to Samir for protection could be okay, but if she figures out how to protect others, she can use that skill for herself.'

But it was the radio incident that taught me an important lesson. It was then that Mother told me about the need to chew my words before letting them out. 'Turn each word around your tongue seven times, with your lips tightly shut, before uttering a sentence,' she said. 'Because once your words are out, you might lose a lot.' Then I remembered how, in one of the tales from *A Thousand and One Nights*, a single misspoken word could bring disaster to the unfortunate one who had pronounced it and displeased the caliph, or king. Sometimes, the *siaf*, or executioner, would even be called in.

However, words could save the person who knew how to string them artfully together. That is what happened to Scheherazade, the author of the thousand and one tales. The king was about to chop off her head, but she was able to stop him at the last minute, just by using words. I was eager to find out how she had done it.

2

Scheherazade, the King, and the Words

One late afternoon, Mother took the time to explain to me why the tales were called *A Thousand and One Nights*. It was no accident because, for each one of those many, many nights, Scheherazade, the young bride, had to spin an entrancing, captivating tale to make her husband, the King, forget his angry plan to execute her at dawn. I was terrorized. 'Mother, do you mean that if the King does not like Scheherazade's story, he will call in his *siaf* (executioner)?' I kept asking for alternatives for the poor girl. I wanted other possibilities. Why could the story displease the King, yet Scheherazade be allowed to live? Why could Scheherazade not just say what she wanted, without having to worry about the King? Or why could she not reverse the situation in the palace, and request that the King tell her a captivating story every night? Then he would realize how frightening it was to have to please someone who had the power to chop off your head. Mother said that I needed to hear the details first; then I could look for escapes.

Scheherazade's marriage to the King, she said, was not a normal one at all. It had taken place under very bad circumstances. King Schahriar had discovered his wife in bed with a slave, and, deeply hurt and enraged, had beheaded them both. To his great amazement, however, he discovered that the double murder was not enough to make him forget his ferocious anger. Revenge became his nightly obsession. He needed to kill more women. So he asked his vizier, the highest official in his court, who also happened to be Scheherazade's father, to bring him a virgin every night. The King would then marry her, stay with her that night, and order her executed at dawn. And so he did for three years, killing more than one thousand innocent girls, 'till folk raised outcry against him and cursed him, praying Allah utterly to destroy him and his rule, and women made an uproar and mothers wept and parents fled with their daughters till there remained not in the city a young person for carnal copulation.'[1] Carnal copulation, explained Mother when Cousin Samir jumped up and down and yelled for an explanation, was when bride and groom lay together in a bed and slept until morning.

Finally, one day, in all the city, there were only two virgins left: Scheherazade, the eldest daughter of the Vizier, and her little sister Duniazad. When the Vizier went home that evening, pale and preoccupied, Scheherazade asked him what was the matter. He told her his problem, and she reacted in a way her father did not expect at all. Instead of begging him to help her escape, she immediately volunteered to go and spend the night with the King. 'I wish thou wouldst give me in marriage to this King

---

[1] Quoted from the wonderful translation, *The Book of the Thousand and One Nights*, by Richard F. Burton. Privately printed by the Burton Club, date of publication unknown (introduction written in 1885), vol. I, p. 14. However, the Burton translation can be confusing at times, with its archaic language. Modern recent translations may be easier for beginners to read.

Schahriar,' she said. 'Either I shall live or I shall be a ransom for the virgin daughters of Muslims and the cause of their deliverance from his hands and thine.'

Scheherazade's father, who loved her dearly, opposed such a plan, and tried to convince her that she had to help him think of another solution. Marrying her off to Schahriar was like condemning her to certain death. But she, unlike her father, was convinced that she had exceptional power and could stop the killing. She would cure the troubled King's soul simply by talking to him about things that had happened to others. She would take him to faraway lands to observe foreign ways, so he could get closer to the strangeness within himself. She would help him see his prison, his obsessive hatred of women. Scheherazade was sure that if she could bring the King to see himself, he would want to change and to love more. Reluctantly, her father gave in, and she was married that very night to Schahriar.[2]

As soon as she entered King Schahriar's bedroom, Scheherazade started telling him such a marvelous story, which she cleverly left hanging at a most suspenseful part, that he could not bear to part with her at dawn. So he let her live until the next night, so she could finish her tale. But on the second night, Scheherazade told him another wonderful story, which she was again far from finishing when dawn arrived, and the King had to let her live again. The same thing happened the next night, and

---

[2] I was amazed to realize that for many Westerners, Scheherazade was considered a lovely but simple-minded entertainer, someone who narrates innocuous tales and dresses fabulously. In our part of the world, Scheherazade is perceived as a courageous heroine and is one of our rare female mythical figures. Scheherazade is a strategist and a powerful thinker, who uses her psychological knowledge of human beings to get them to walk faster and leap higher. Like Saladin and Sindbad, she makes us bolder and more sure of ourselves and of our capacity to transform the world and its people.

the next, for a thousand nights, which is almost three years, until the King was unable to imagine living without her. By then, they already had two children, and after a thousand and one nights, he renounced his terrible habit of chopping off women's heads.

When Mother finished Scheherazade's story, I cried, 'But how does one learn how to tell stories which please kings?' Mother mumbled, as if talking to herself, that that was a woman's lifetime work. This reply did not help me much, of course, but then she added that all I needed to know for the moment was that my chances of happiness would depend upon how skillful I became with words. With this knowledge, Samir and I (who had already decided to avoid upsetting the grownups with unwelcomed words, thanks to the radio incident) started training ourselves. We would sit for hours, silently practicing, chewing words, and turning them seven times around our tongues, all the while watching the grownups to see if they were noticing anything.

But the grownups never noticed anything, especially on the courtyard level, where life was very proper and strict. Only upstairs were things less rigid. There, divorced and widowed aunts, relatives, and their children, occupied a maze of small rooms. The number of relatives living with us at any one time varied according to the amount of conflict in their lives. Distant female relatives would sometimes come to seek refuge on our top floors for a few weeks when they got into fights with their husbands. Some would come to stay, with their children, for a short time only, just to show their husbands that they had another place to stay, that they could survive on their own and were not desperately dependent. (This strategy often was successful, and they would return home in a stronger bargaining position.) But other relatives came to stay for good, after a divorce or some other serious problem, and this was one of the traditions Father always worried about whenever someone attacked the institution of harem life. 'Where will the troubled women go?' he would say.

The rooms upstairs were very simple with white tiled floors, whitewashed walls, and sparse furniture. Very narrow sofas, upholstered with multi-flowered peasant cottons and cushions, were scattered here and there, along with easily washable raffia mats. Wet feet, slippers, and even the occasional spilled cup of tea, did not produce the same excessive reactions up here as they did downstairs. Life upstairs was so much easier, especially since everything was also accompanied by *hanan*, a Moroccan emotional quality that I rarely have encountered elsewhere. *Hanan* is hard to define exactly, but basically, it is a free-flowing, easygoing, unconditionally available tenderness. People who give *hanan*, like Aunt Habiba, never threaten to withdraw their love when you commit some unintentional minor or even major infraction. *Hanan* was hard to come by downstairs, especially among the mothers, who were too busy teaching you to respect the frontier to bother with tenderness.

Upstairs was also the place to go for storytelling. You would climb the hundreds of glazed steps that led all the way up to the third and top floor of the house, and the terrace which lay before it, all whitewashed, spacious, and inviting. That was where Aunt Habiba had her room, small and quite empty. Her husband had kept everything from their marriage, with the idea that should he ever lift his finger and ask her to come home again, she would bow her head and come rushing back. 'But he can never take the most important things away from me,' Aunt Habiba would say sometimes, 'my laughter and all the wonderful stories I can tell when the audience is worth it.' I once asked Cousin Malika what our aunt meant by 'an audience who is worth it,' and she confessed that she did not know either. I said maybe we should ask her directly, but Malika said no, better not, because Aunt

Habiba might start crying. Aunt Habiba often cried for no reason; everyone said so. But we loved her, and could hardly sleep on Thursday nights, so excited were we at the prospect of her Friday storytelling sessions. These gatherings usually ended in great confusion, because they lasted too long, according to our mothers, who were often forced to climb up all those stairs to fetch us. And then we would scream, and the most spoiled of my cousins, like Samir, would roll on the floor, and shout that they did not feel sleepy, not at all.

But if you did manage to stay until the story ended, that is until the heroine triumphed over her enemies and crossed back over the 'seven rivers, seven mountains, and seven seas,' you were faced with yet another problem: you were scared to go back down the stairs. First of all, there was no light. The switches to the stair lights were all controlled by Ahmed, the doorkeeper, from the entrance gate. He turned them off at 9 P.M., to signal that everyone on the terrace was going in and all traffic ought to be officially stopped. The second problem was that a whole population of *djinnis* (demons) was out there, lurking in silence and waiting to jump out at you. And last, but not the least, was the fact that Cousin Samir was so good at imitating the *djinnis* that I often mistook him for the real thing. Several times, I literally had to feign passing out to get him to stop from posing as a *djinni*.

Sometimes, when the story lasted for hours, the mothers did not appear, and the whole house fell suddenly silent, we would beg Aunt Habiba to let us spend the night with her. She would unfold her beautiful bridal carpet, the one she kept carefully folded behind her cedar chest, and cover it with a clean white sheet and perfume it with orange-flower water, special for the occasion. She did not have enough cushions for all of us to use as pillows, but that was not a problem, as we did not care. She would share with us her huge, heavy wool blanket, turn off the electric light, and place a big candle on the threshold at our feet. 'If by any chance someone needs to go urgently to the toilet,' she would say, 'remember that this carpet is one of the only things I have which reminds me of my previous life as a happily married lady.'

So, on these graceful nights, we would fall asleep listening to our aunt's voice opening up magic glass doors, leading to moonlit meadows. And when we awoke in the morning, the whole city lay at our feet. Aunt Habiba had a small room, but a large window with a view that reached as far as the Northern mountains.

She knew how to talk in the night. With words alone, she could put us onto a large ship sailing from Aden to the Maldives, or take us to an island where the birds spoke like human beings. Riding on her words, we traveled past Sind and Hind (India), leaving Muslim territories behind, living dangerously, and making friends with Christians and Jews, who shared their bizarre foods with us and watched us do our prayers, while we watched them do theirs. Sometimes we traveled so far that no gods were to be found, only sun- and fire-worshippers, but even they seemed friendly and endearing when introduced by Aunt Habiba. Her tales made me long to become an adult and an expert storyteller myself. I wanted to learn how to talk in the night.

3

The French Harem

Our house gate was a definite *hudud*, or frontier, because you needed permission to step in or out. Every move had to be justified and even getting to the gate was a procedure. If you were coming from the courtyard, you had to first walk down an endless corridor, and then you came face to face with Ahmed, the doorkeeper, who was usually sitting on his throne-like sofa, always with his tea tray by his side, ready to entertain. Since the right of passage always involved a rather elaborate negotiating process, you were invited either to sit beside him on his impressive sofa, or to face him, duly relaxed on the out-of-place 'fauteuil d'França', his hard, shabby, upholstered easy chair that he had picked out for himself on a rare visit to the *joutya*, or local flea market. Ahmed often had the youngest of his five children on his lap, because he took care of them whenever his wife Luza went to work. She was a first-rate cook and accepted occasional assignments outside our home when the money was good.

Our house gate was a gigantic stone arch with impressive

carved wooden doors. It separated the women's harem from the male strangers walking in the streets. (Uncle's and Father's honor and prestige depended on that separation, we were told.) Children could step out of the gate, if their parents permitted it, but not grownup women. 'I would wake up at dawn,' Mother would say now and then. 'If I only could go for a walk in the early morning when the streets are deserted. The light must be blue then, or maybe pink, like at sunset. What is the color of the morning in the deserted, silent streets?' No one answered her questions. In a harem, you don't necessarily ask questions to get answers. You ask questions just to understand what is happening to you. Roaming freely in the streets was every woman's dream. Aunt Habiba's most popular tale, which she narrated on special occasions only, was about 'The Woman with Wings,' who could fly away from the courtyard whenever she wanted to. Every time Aunt Habiba told that story, the women in the courtyard would tuck their caftans into their belts, and dance away with their arms spread wide as if they were about to fly. Cousin Chama, who was seventeen, had me confused for years, because she managed to convince me that all women had invisible wings, and that mine would develop too, when I was older.

Our house gate also protected us from the foreigners standing a few meters away, at another equally busy and dangerous frontier – the one that separated our old city, the Medina, from the new French city, the Ville Nouvelle. My cousins and I would sometimes slip out of the gate when Ahmed was busy talking or napping, to take a look at the French soldiers. They dressed in blue uniforms, wore rifles on their shoulders, and had small gray eyes that were always alert. They often tried to talk to us children, because the adults never spoke with them, but we were instructed never to answer back. We knew that the French were greedy and had come a long way to conquer our land, even though Allah had already given them a beautiful one, with bustling cities, thick forests, luscious green fields, and cows much bigger than ours that gave four times as much milk. But somehow the French needed to get more.

Because we lived on the frontier between the old city and the new, we could see how different the French Ville Nouvelle was from our Medina. Their streets were large and straight, and lit by bright lights in the night. (Father said that they squandered Allah's energy because people did not need that much bright light in a safe community.) They also had fast cars. Our Medina streets were narrow, dark, and serpentine – filled with so many twists and turns that cars could not enter, and foreigners could not find their way out if they ever dared to come in. This was the real reason the French had to build a new city for themselves: they were afraid to live in ours.

Most people walked on foot in the Medina. Father and Uncle had their mules, but poor people like Ahmed had only donkeys, and children and women had to walk. The French were afraid to walk. They were always in their cars. Even the soldiers would stay in their cars when things got bad. Their fear was quite an amazing thing to us children, because we saw that grownups could be as afraid as we could. And these grownups who were afraid were on the outside, supposedly free. The powerful ones who had created the frontier were also the fearful ones. The Ville Nouvelle was like their harem; just like women, they could not walk freely in the Medina. So you could be powerful, and still be the prisoner of a frontier.

Nonetheless, the French soldiers, who often looked so very young, afraid, and lonely at their posts, terrorized the entire Medina. They had power and could hurt us.

One day in January 1944, Mother said, King Mohammed V, backed by nationalists all over Morocco, went to the top-ranking French colonial administrator, the Résident Général, to make a formal demand for independence. The Résident Général got very upset. How dare you Moroccans ask for independence! he must have screamed, and to punish us, he launched his soldiers into the Medina. Armored cars forced their way as far as they could into the serpentine streets. People turned to Mecca to pray. Thousands of men recited the anxiety prayer, consisting of one single word repeated over and over for hours when one is faced with disaster: '*Ya Latif, Ya Latif, Ya Latif!*' (O Sensitive One!) *Latif* is one of the hundred names of Allah, and Aunt Habiba often said it was the most beautiful one of all because it describes Allah as a source of tender sympathy, who feels your sorrow and can help you. But the armed French soldiers, trapped in the narrow streets, surrounded by chants of '*Ya Latif*' repeated thousands of times, became nervous and lost control. They started shooting at the praying crowds and within minutes, corpses were falling on top of each other on the mosque's doorstep, while the chants were still going on inside. Mother said that Samir and I were barely four at the time and no one noticed us watching from our gate as the blood-soaked corpses, all dressed in the ceremonial white prayer *djellaba*, were carried back home. 'For months afterward, you and Samir had nightmares,' she said, 'and you could not even see the color red without running to hide. We had to take you to the Moulay Driss sanctuary many Fridays in a row to have the *sharifs* (holy men) perform protection rituals over you, and I had to put a Koranic amulet under your pillow for a whole year before you slept normally again.' After that tragic day, the French walked around carrying guns with them in plain view all the time, while Father had to ask permission from many different sources just to keep his hunting rifle, and even then, had to keep it concealed unless he was in the forest.

All these events puzzled me and I talked about them often with Yasmina, my maternal grandmother, who lived on a beautiful farm with cows and sheep and endless fields of flowers, one hundred kilometers to the west of us, between Fez and the

Ocean. We visited her once a year, and I would talk to her about frontiers and fears and differences, and the why of it all. Yasmina knew a lot about fear, all kinds of fears. 'I am an expert on fear, Fatima,' she would tell me, caressing my forehead as I played with her pearls and pink beads, 'And I will tell you things when you are older. I will teach you how to get over fears.'

Often, I could not sleep the first few nights on Yasmina's farm – the frontiers were not clear enough. There were no closed gates to be seen anywhere, only wide, flat, open fields where flowers grew and animals wandered peaceably about. But Yasmina explained to me that the farm was part of Allah's original earth, which had no frontiers, just vast, open fields without borders or boundaries, and that I should not be afraid. But how could I walk in an open field without being attacked? I kept asking. And then Yasmina created a game that I loved, to help put me to sleep, called *mshia-f-lekhla* (the walk in the open fields). She would hold me tight as I lay down, and I would clasp her beads with my two hands, close my eyes, and imagine myself walking through an endless field of flowers. 'Step lightly,' Yasmina would say, 'so you can hear the flowers' song. They are whispering, "*salam, salam*" (peace, peace).' I would repeat the flowers' refrain as fast as I could, all danger would disappear, and I would fall asleep. '*Salam, salam,*' murmured the flowers, Yasmina, and I. And the next thing I knew, it was morning and I was lying in Yasmina's big brass bed, with my hands full of pearls and pink beads. From outside came the mixed music of breezes touching the leaves and birds talking to one another, and no one was in sight but King Farouk, the peacock, and Thor, the fat white duck.

Actually, Thor was also the name of Yasmina's most hated co-wife, but I could only call the woman Thor when thinking about her silently to myself. When I said her name out loud, I had to call her Lalla Thor. *Lalla* is our title of respect for all important women, just as *Sidi* is our title of respect for all important men. As a child, I had to call all important grownups Lalla and Sidi, and kiss their hands at sunset, when the lights were turned on and we said *msakum* (good evening). Every evening, Samir and I would kiss everyone's hands as quickly as we could so we could return to our games without hearing the nasty remark, 'Tradition is being lost.' We got so good at it that we managed to rush through the ritual at an incredible speed, but sometimes, we were in such a hurry that we would trip over each other and collapse onto the laps of important people, or even fall down on the carpet. Then everyone would start laughing. Mother would laugh until there were tears in her eyes. 'Poor dears,' she would say, 'they already are tired of kissing hands, and it is only the beginning.'

But Lalla Thor on the farm, just like Lalla Mani in Fez, never laughed. She was always very serious, proper, and correct. As the first wife of Grandfather Tazi, she had a very important position in the family. She also had no housekeeping duties, and was very rich, two privileges that Yasmina could not abide. 'I could not care how rich this woman is,' she would say, 'she ought to be working like all the rest of us. Are we Muslims or not? If we are, everyone is equal. Allah said so. His prophet preached the same.' Yasmina said that I should never accept inequality, for it was not logical. That was why she named her fat white duck Lalla Thor.

4

Yasmina's First Co-Wife

When Lalla Thor heard that Yasmina had named a duck after her, she was outraged. She summoned Grandfather Tazi to her salon, which was actually a self-contained palace, with an internal garden, a large fountain, and a glorious ten-meter-long wall covered with Venetian glass. Grandfather came in reluctantly, walking with long strides and holding a Koran in his hand, as if to show that he had been interrupted in his reading. He was wearing his usual loose white cotton pants, his white cotton chiffon *qamis* and *farajiya*, and his yellow leather slippers.[1] In the

---

[1] In the 1940s, most Moroccan men and women in the cities dressed identically, with three layers of robes. The first layer, the *qamis*, was very soft, made of a natural fiber such as cotton or silk. The second layer, the caftan, was made of heavy wool and was discarded in the spring, when the weather got warm. The third, outer layer was the *farajiya*, a thin, often sheer robe, slit on the sides and worn over the caftan. When men and women stepped out in public, they added a fourth layer, the *djellaba*, a long, loose-fitting robe.

house, he never wore a *djellaba*, except when hosting visitors.

Physically, Grandfather had the typical look of the Northerners of the Rif region, where his family had originated. He was tall and lanky, with an angular face, fair skin, light and rather small eyes, and a very distant, haughty air. People from the Rif are proud and not very talkative, and Grandfather hated it when his wives argued or provoked conflict of any kind. Once, he stopped speaking to Yasmina for a whole year, leaving the room whenever she entered it, because she had instigated two disputes in a single month. After that, she could not afford to be involved in more than one fight every three years. This time it was the duck, and the whole farm was alerted.

Lalla Thor offered Grandfather tea before attacking the subject. Then she threatened to leave him if the duck's name was not changed at once. It was the eve of a religious festival, and Lalla Thor was dressed to the hilt, wearing her tiara and her legendary caftan, embroidered with genuine pearls and garnets, to remind everyone of her privileged status. But Grandfather was apparently quite amused by the whole affair because he smiled when the subject of the duck came up. He had always found Yasmina to be quite eccentric, and had in fact needed a long time to get used to some of her habits, such as climbing up trees, and

With independence in the 1950s, however, clothing styles in Morocco underwent a revolution. First, both men and women started wearing Western garb on occasion. Then, the traditional dress itself was transformed and adapted to modern times. The era of individualized and innovative clothing had begun, and today, if you observe a Moroccan city street, you will notice that no two people dress alike. Men and women borrow from each other, and from the rest of Africa, and from the West. For example, bright colors, which were once a woman's prerogative only, are now also worn by men. Women borrow the men's *djellabas* and men borrow the women's *boubous*, the large, floating, embroidered robes that come from Senegal and other black Muslim countries. And young Moroccan women have even been creating unheard-of sexy mini-*djellabas* out of Italian-inspired knits.

hanging up there for hours at a time. Sometimes, she even managed to talk a few co-wives into joining her, and then they would have tea served all around while sitting on the branches. But what always saved Yasmina was the fact that she made Grandfather laugh, and that was a real achievement, for he was a rather moody person. Now, caught in Lalla Thor's luxurious salon, Grandfather slyly suggested that she retaliate by naming her ugly dog Yasmina – 'That would force the rebel to rename her duck.' But Lalla Thor was in no mood for jokes. 'You are completely under Yasmina's spell,' she shouted. 'If you let her get away with this today, tomorrow she will buy a donkey and name it Sidi Tazi. This woman does not respect hierarchies. She is a troublemaker, like everyone from the Atlas Mountains, and she is bringing chaos to this decent house. Either she gives her duck another name, or I am leaving. I don't understand the influence she has on you. It's not as if she were beautiful – she's so skinny and so tall. Like an ugly giraffe.'

It was true that Yasmina did not fit the beauty standards of her day, of which Lalla Thor was a perfect model. Lalla Thor had very white skin, a round face like the full moon, and a lot of flesh all around, especially on her hips and buttocks and bust. Yasmina, on the other hand, had the brown, suntanned skin of mountaineers, a long face with strikingly high cheek bones, and hardly any bust. She stood almost 180 centimeters tall, which was just a little shorter than Grandfather, and had the longest legs you've ever seen, which was why she was so good at climbing trees and performing all kinds of acrobatic stunts. But her legs did look like sticks under her caftan. To camouflage them, she sewed herself an enormous pair of *sarwals*, or harem pants, with many pleats. She also cut long slits in the sides of her short caftan to give herself some volume. At first, Lalla Thor tried to get everyone to laugh at Yasmina's innovative dress, but very soon all the other co-wives were imitating the rebel because the slit, shortened caftans gave them a lot more freedom of movement.

When Grandfather went to Yasmina to complain about the duck, she showed little sympathy. So what if Lalla Thor did leave? she said; he would never feel lonely. 'You will still have eight concubines to take care of you!' So Grandfather tried to bribe Yasmina by offering her a heavy silver bracelet from Tiznit, in exchange for which she had to make a couscous with her duck. Yasmina kept the bracelet, and told him that she needed a few days to think things over. Then, the following Friday, she came back with a counterproposal. She could not possibly kill the duck, because its name was Lalla Thor! It would not be a good omen. However, she could promise never to call her duck by its name in public. She would do so only in her mind. From then on, I was instructed to do the same and I worked very hard to keep the duck's name to myself.

Then there was the story of King Farouk, the farm peacock. Who would name a peacock after the famous ruler of Egypt? What was the pharaoh doing on the farm? Well you see, Yasmina and her co-wives did not like the Egyptian King, for he kept threatening to repudiate his lovely wife, Princess Farida (whom he did eventually divorce in January 1948). Just what had brought the couple to this impasse? What unforgivable crime had she commited? She had given birth to three daughters, none of whom could accede to the throne.

According to Muslim law, a woman cannot rule a country, although that had happened a few centuries ago, Grandmother said. With the help of the Turkish army, Shajarat al-Durr had acceded to the throne of Egypt after the death of her husband, Sultan al-Salih. She was a concubine, a slave of Turkish origin, and she ruled for four months, governing neither better nor worse than the men who came before and after her.[2] But of course, not all Muslim women are as astute or as cruel as Shajarat al-Durr. When Shajarat al-Durr's second husband decided to take a second wife, for example, she waited until he got into the *hammam*, or bath, to relax, and then 'forgot' to open the door. Of course he died from the steam and the heat. But poor Princess Farida was not such a perfect criminal, and she did not know how to maneuver in power circles or defend her rights in the palace. She was of very modest origins, and was somewhat helpless, too, which was why the co-wives on the farm, who had similar backgrounds to hers, loved her and suffered for her humiliations. There is nothing so humiliating for a woman, Yasmina said, as being cast out. 'Shlup! Right into the street like a cat. Is that a decent way to treat a woman?'

Besides, Yasmina added, as high and mighty as King Farouk was, he did not know much about how babies were made. 'If he did,' she said, 'he would know that his wife was not responsible for not having a boy. You need two to make a baby.' And she was right about that, I knew. To make babies, the bride and the groom had to dress up nicely, put flowers in their hair, and lie down together on a very big bed. The next thing you knew, many mornings later, there was a little baby crawling between them.

The farm kept track of King Farouk's conjugal caprices through Radio Cairo, and Yasmina's condemnation of him was swift and decisive. 'What kind of good Muslim leader,' she said, 'dismisses a wife just because she does not produce a son? Allah alone, says the Koran, is responsible for the sex of babies. In a justly run Muslim Cairo, King Farouk would be dismissed from the throne! Poor, lovely princess Farida! Sacrificed through sheer ignorance and vanity. Egyptians should repudiate their king.'

[2] Shajarat al-Durr took power in the year 648 of the Muslim calendar (A.D. 1250).

And that is how the farm peacock came to be called King Farouk. But if condemning kings was an easy matter for Yasmina, dealing with a powerful co-wife was another matter altogether, even after already having gotten away with naming a duck after her rival.

Lalla Thor was powerful, and she was the only aristocratic, city-born wife of Grandfather Tazi. Her last name also was Tazi, as she was one of his cousins, and she had brought with her, as a dowry, a tiara of emeralds, sapphires, and gray pearls, which was kept in the big strongbox in the right-hand corner of the men's salon. But Yasmina, who was from a modest rural background like all the other co-wives, was not impressed. 'I can't consider someone superior just because she owns a tiara,' she said. 'Besides, as rich as she is, she is still stuck in a harem, just like me.' I asked Yasmina what that meant, to be stuck in a harem, and she gave me several different answers, which of course only confused me.

Sometimes, she said that to be stuck in a harem simply meant that a woman had lost her freedom of movement. Other times, she said that a harem meant misfortune because a woman had to share her husband with many others. Yasmina herself had to share Grandfather with eight co-wives, which meant that she had to sleep alone for eight nights before she could hug and snuggle with him for one. 'And hugging and snuggling your husband is wonderful,' she said.[3] 'I am so happy your generation will not

---

[3] At this stage, it would perhaps be helpful to introduce a distinction between two kinds of harems: the first we will call imperial harems, and the second, domestic harems. The first flourished with the territorial conquests and accumulation of wealth of the Muslim imperial dynasties, starting with the Omayyads, a seventh-century Arab dynasty based in Damascus, and ending with the Ottomans, a Turkish dynasty which threatened European capitals from the sixteenth century onward until its last sultan, Abdelhamid II, was deposed by western powers in 1909, and his harem dismantled. We

have to share husbands anymore.'

The nationalists, who were fighting the French, had promised

will call domestic harems those which continued to exist after 1909, when Muslims lost power and their territories were occupied and colonized. Domestic harems were in fact extended families, like the one described in this book, with no slaves and no eunuchs, and often with monogamous couples, but who carried on the tradition of women's seclusion. (Muslims in principle were never supposed to castrate boys, since such operations were highly censored by Islam, which forbids altering God's creation. They were supposed to buy Christians and Jews who would perform castration. Records reporting such commercial transactions exist, but there always exists a wide gap between principles and reality.)

It is the Ottoman imperial harem that has fascinated the West almost to the point of obsession. It is this Turkish harem which inspired hundreds of orientalist paintings of the eighteenth, nineteenth, and twentieth centuries, such as Ingres's famous 'Bain Turc' (1862), or Delacroix's 'Femmes Turques au Bain' (1854), or John Frederick Lewis's 'In the Bey's Garden' (1865). Imperial harems, that is, splendid palaces full of luxuriously dressed and lasciviously reclined indolent women, with slaves standing by and eunuchs watching the gates, existed when the emperor, his Wazir, generals, tax collectors, etc., had enough influence and money to buy hundreds and sometimes thousands of slaves from conquered territories, and then provide for such expensive households. Why have the Ottoman imperial harems had such an impact on Western imagination? One reason could be the Ottoman's spectacular conquest of Constantinople, the Byzantine capital, in 1453, and their subsequent occupation of many European cities, as well as the fact that they were the West's closest and most threatening neighbor.

By contrast, domestic harems, that is, those which continued to exist in the Muslim world after its colonization by the West, are rather dull, for they have a strong bourgeois dimension and, as is said above, are more of an extended family, with hardly any erotic dimension to speak of. In these domestic harems, a man and his sons and their wives lived in the same house, pooled their resources, and requested that the women refrain from stepping outside. The men need not have many wives, as is the case in the harem which inspired the tales in this book. What defines it as a harem is not polygamy, but the men's desire to seclude their wives, and their wish to maintain an extended household rather than break into nuclear units.

to create a new Morocco, with equality for all. Every woman was to have the same right to education as a man, as well as the right to enjoy monogamy – a privileged, exclusive relationship with her husband. In fact, many of the nationalist leaders and their followers in Fez already had only one wife, and looked down on those who had many. Father and Uncle, who espoused the nationalist views, each had only one wife.

The nationalists also were against slavery. Slavery had been prevalent in Morocco at the beginning of the century, Yasmina said, even after the French had made it illegal, and many of her co-wives had been bought in slave markets. (Yasmina also said that all human beings were equal, no matter how much money they had, where they came from, what place they held in the hierarchy, or what their religion or language was. If you had two eyes, one nose, two legs, and two hands, then you were equal to everyone else. I reminded her that if we counted a dog's forelegs as hands, he would be our equal too, and she immediately responded with, 'But of course he is our equal! Animals are just like us; the only thing they lack is speech.')

Some of Yasmina's co-wives who had been slaves had come from foreign lands like the Sudan, but others had been stolen from their parents right in Morocco, during the chaos that ensued after the arrival of the French in 1912. When the Makhzen, or the State, does not express the will of the people, Yasmina said, women always pay a high price, because insecurity and violence set in. That's exactly what happened then. The Makhzen and its officials, unable to face the French armies, signed the treaty which gave France the right to rule Morocco as a protectorate but the people refused to give up. Resistance sprang up in the mountains and the deserts, and civil war crept in.

'You had heroes,' Yasmina said, 'but you also had all kinds of armed criminals running around all over. The first were fighting the French, while the second were robbing the people. In the South, at the edge of the Sahara, you had heroes such as Al-Hiba, and later his brother, who resisted until 1934. In my region, the Atlas, the proud Moha ou Hamou Zayani kept the French army at bay until 1920. In the North, the prince of the fighters, Abdelkrim, gave the French – and the Spanish – a real beating, until they ganged up on him and defeated him in 1926. But also, during all this turmoil, little girls were being stolen from their poor parents in the mountains and sold in the big cities to rich men. It was standard practice. Your grandfather was a nice man, but he bought slaves. It was the natural thing to do back then. Now he has changed, and like most of the notables in the big cities, he supports the nationalists' ideals, including respect for the individual, monogamy, the abolition of slavery, and so on. Yet strangely enough, we co-wives feel closer to one another than ever, although those who were slaves among us have tried to track down and contact their original families. We feel like sisters; our real family is the one that we have woven around your Grandfather. I could even imagine changing my mind about Lalla Thor, if she ever stopped looking down on all of us because we don't have tiaras.'

Naming the duck Lalla Thor was Yasmina's way of participating in the creation of the beautiful, new Morocco, the Morocco that I, her little granddaughter, was going to step into. 'Morocco has changed quickly, little girl,' she often told me, 'and it will keep on doing so.' That prediction made me feel very happy. I was going to grow up in a wonderful kingdom where women had rights, including the freedom to snuggle up with their own husbands every night. But even though Yasmina lamented having to wait eight nights for her husband, she added that she should not complain too much, because the wives of Harun al-Rashid, the Abbasid Caliph of Baghdad, each had had to wait nine hundred and ninety-nine nights, for he had one thousand *jaryas*, or slave girls. 'To wait eight nights is not like waiting nine hundred and ninety-nine nights,' she said. 'That is almost three years! So things are getting better. Soon, we will have one man, one wife.[4] Let's go feed the birds. We'll have lots of time later to talk more about harems.' And then we would rush to her garden to feed the birds.

[4] In fact, the law never did change. Today, almost half a century later, Muslim women still are fighting to have polygamy banned. But legislators, all men, say it is *shari'a* law, religious law, and cannot be changed. In the summer of 1992, a Moroccan women's association (L'Union d'Action Feminine, whose president, Lahfa Jbabdi, is a brilliant sociologist and journalist) that had collected one million signatures against polygamy and divorce became the target of the fundamentalist press, which issued a *fatwa* (a legal advice given by an expert in Islamic religious sciences) calling for the women's execution as heretics. Indeed, when it comes to the status of women, one could say that the Muslim world has regressed since Grandmother's time. The fundamentalist press's defense of polygamy and divorce is in fact an attack against the right of women to participate in the law-making process. Most Muslim governments, and their fundamentalist oppositions, even those that call themselves modern, keep polygamy in the family law codes, not because it is particularly widespread but because they want to show women that their needs are not important. The law is not there to serve them, nor to guarantee their right to happiness and emotional security. The prevailing belief is that women and the law do not belong together, women ought to accept men's law, because they cannot change it. The suppression of a man's right to polygamy would mean that women have their say in the law, that society is not run by and for men's whims alone. Where a Muslim government stands on the question of polygamy is a good way to measure the degree to which it has accepted democratic ideas. And if we do take it as an indicator of democracy, we see that very few Muslim countries are up-to-date on human rights. Tunisia and Turkey are the most progressive.

5

Chama and the Caliph

'What exactly is a harem?' was not the kind of question grown-ups volunteered to answer. Yet they were always insisting that we children use precise words. Every word, they kept saying, has a specific meaning and you ought to use it for that specific one only, and for none other. But, given a choice, I would have used different words for Yasmina's harem and our own, so different were they. Yasmina's harem was an open farm with no visible high walls. Ours in Fez was like a fortress. Yasmina and her co-wives rode horses, swam in the river, caught fish, and cooked it over open fires. Mother could not even step out of the gate without asking multiple permissions, and even then, all she could do was visit the shrine of Moulay Driss (the patron saint of the city) or her brother who happened to live down the street, or attend a religious festival. And poor Mother always had to be accompanied by other women of the household, and by one of my young male cousins. So it did not make sense to me to use the same word for both Yasmina's and Mother's situations.

But whenever I tried to find out more about the word 'harem,' bitter arguments ensued. You needed only to pronounce the word, and impolite remarks would start to fly. Samir and I discussed this matter, and concluded that if words in general were dangerous, then 'harem' in particular was explosive. Anytime someone wanted to start a war in the courtyard, all she had to do was prepare some tea, invite a few people to sit down, throw out the word 'harem', and wait for half an hour or so. Then poised, elegant ladies, dressed in lovely embroidered silk caftans and pearl-studded slippers, suddenly would turn into shrieking furies. Samir and I therefore decided that, as children, it was our duty to protect the adults. We would handle the word 'harem' with parsimony, and gather our information through discretion and observation only.

One grownup camp said that the harem was a good thing, while the other said that it was bad. Grandmother Lalla Mani and Chama's mother, Lalla Radia, belonged to the pro-harem camp; Mother, Chama, and Aunt Habiba, to the anti-harem one. Grandmother Lalla Mani often got the discussion started by saying that if the women were not separated from the men, society would come to a halt and work would not get done. 'If women were free to run about in the streets,' she said, 'men would stop working because they would want to have fun.' And unfortunately, she went on, fun did not help a society produce the food and goods it needed to survive. So, if famine were to be avoided, women had to stay in their place at home.

Later, Samir and I had a long consultation about the word 'fun' and we decided that, when used by grownups, it had to do with sex. We wanted to be absolutely clear about that though, and so we took the matter to Cousin Malika. She said that we were definitely right. Then we asked her, standing as tall as we could, 'What *is* sex, according to you?' Not that we did not already know the answer, we just wanted to make sure. But Malika, who thought we knew nothing, solemnly pushed back her braids, sat down on a sofa, took a cushion in her lap like grownups do when they are reflecting, and said slowly, 'The first night of the marriage celebration, when everyone goes to sleep, the bride and groom stay by themselves in their bedroom. The groom makes the bride sit down on the bed, they hold hands, and he tries to make her look at him straight in the eyes. But the bride resists, she keeps her eyes down. That is very important. The bride is very shy and frightened. The groom says a poem. The bride listens with her eyes glued to the floor, and finally she smiles. Then he kisses her on the forehead. She still keeps her eyes down. He gives her a cup of tea. She starts drinking it slowly. He takes the cup away, sits near her, and kisses her.'

Malika, who shamelessly manipulated our curiosity, decided to pause right there at the kiss, knowing that Samir and I were dying to know where the groom actually kissed the bride. Kissing on the forehead, cheek, and hand meant nothing unusual, but the mouth was indeed another story. However, we decided to teach Malika a lesson, and instead of showing our curiosity, Samir and I started whispering to each other, oblivious of her existence altogether. Showing total disinterest to your speaker, Aunt Habiba had recently told us, was one good way for the weak to take power: 'To speak while others are listening is indeed the expression of power itself. But even the seemingly subservient, silent listener has an extremely strategic role, that of the audience. What if the powerful speaker loses his audience?'

And sure enough, Malika immediately resumed her dissertation on what happens on the bridal night. 'The groom kisses the bride on the mouth. Then they both lie together in a big bed, with no one looking.' We did not ask any more questions after that. We knew all the rest. The man and the woman take off their clothes, shut their eyes, and the baby follows a few months later.

The harem makes it impossible for men and women to see

each other, so everybody proceeds with their duties. While Lalla Mani was praising harem life, Aunt Habiba would be fuming; you could tell by the way she kept readjusting her headdress even though it was not slipping. Because she was divorced, however, she could not contradict Lalla Mani openly, but had to mumble her objections softly to herself, and leave it up to Mother and Chama to voice dissent. Only those who had power could openly correct others and contradict their views. A divorced woman did not have a home really, and had to buy off her presence by making herself as inconspicuous as possible. Aunt Habiba never wore bright colors, for example, even though she sometimes expressed the wish to try on her red silk *farajiya* again. But she never did. Most of the time, she just wore washed-out gray or beige colors, and the only make-up she used was kohl around the eyes. 'The weak have to be disciplined so as to avoid humiliation,' she would say. 'Never let others remind you of your limits. You can be poor, but elegance is always there to be grabbed.'

Mother would begin her attack on Lalla Mani's views by tucking her legs in under her on the sofa, straightening her back, and pulling a cushion onto her lap. She would then cross her arms and stare straight at Lalla Mani. 'The French do not imprison their wives behind walls, my dear mother in-law,' she would say. 'They let them run wild in the local *souk* (market), and everyone has fun, and still the work gets done. In fact, so much work gets done that they can afford to equip strong armies and come down here to shoot at us.'

Then, before Lalla Mani could gather herself together for a counterattack, Chama would present her theory about how the first harem got started. That is when things used to get really bad, because both Lalla Mani and Chama's mother would start screaming that now our ancestors were being insulted, our sacred traditions ridiculed.

44

Chama's theory was actually quite interesting, and Samir and I loved it. Once upon a time, she argued, men fought each other constantly. There was much needless bloodshed, and so one day, they decided to appoint a sultan who would organize things, exercise *sulta*, or authority, and tell the others what to do. All the rest would have to obey. 'But how shall we decide who among us shall be this sultan?' the men wondered as they met to ponder this problem. They reflected very hard and then one of them had an idea. 'The sultan must have something the others do not have,' he said. They reflected some more, and then another man had another idea. 'We should organize a race to catch women,' he suggested, 'And the man who catches the most women will be appointed sultan.'

That's an excellent idea, the men agreed, but what about proof? 'When we all start running in the forest to catch women, we will get dispersed. We need a way to paralyze the women once they're caught, so we can count them, and decide who is the winner.' And that was how the idea of building houses got started. Houses with gates and locks were needed to contain the women. Samir suggested that it might have been simpler just to tie the women to trees, since they had such long braids, but Chama said that in the old days, women were very strong from running in the woods just like men, and if you tied two or three of them to a tree, they might uproot it. Besides, it took too much time and energy to tie up strong women, and they might scratch your face or kick you in some unmentionable place. Building walls and shoving them in was much more handy. And so the men did.

The race was organized all over the world, and the Byzantines won the first round.[1] The Byzantines, who were the nastiest of

---

[1] For an entertaining glimpse at harems in the Roman Empire, see

all the Romans, lived close to the Arabs in the Eastern Mediterranean, where they never missed an occasion to humiliate their neighbors. The Emperor of the Byzantines conquered the world, caught a huge number of women, and put them in his harem to prove that he was the chief. East and West bowed to him. East and West were scared of him. But then, centuries went by and the Arabs started learning how to conquer territories and chase women. They became very good at it and dreamt of conquering the Byzantines. Finally, Caliph Harun al-Rashid had that privilege. He defeated the Roman Emperor in the Muslim year 181 (A.D. 798), and then went on to conquer other parts of the world. When he had gathered one thousand *jarya*, or slave girls, in his harem, he built a big palace in Baghdad and put them in it, so no one would doubt that he was the Sultan. The Arabs became sultans of the world, and they gathered more women. Caliph Al-Mutawwakil gathered four thousand. Al-Muqtadir managed to round up eleven thousand.[2] Everyone was very impressed after that – the Arabs gave orders, the Romans bowed.

But while the Arabs were busy locking women behind doors, the Romans and the other Christians got together and decided to change the rules of the power game in the Mediterranean. Collecting women, they declared, was not relevant anymore. From now on, the sultan would be the one who could build the

Goddesses, Whores, Wives, and Slaves: Women in Classical Antiquity by Sarah B. Pomeroy, Schocken Books, 1975.

[2] The Abbasid Dynasty, the second dynasty of the Muslim Empire, lasted five hundred years, from 132 to 656 of the Muslim calendar (A.D. 750–1258). It ended when the Mongols destroyed Baghdad and killed the Caliph. Harun al-Rashid was the fifth Caliph of the Abbasid Dynasty; he ruled between A.D. 786 and 809. His conquests became legendary, and his reign is regarded as the epitomy of the Muslim golden age. Caliph Al-Mutawwakil was the tenth ruler of the dynasty (A.D. 847–861); Caliph Al-Muqtadir, the nineteenth (A.D. 908–932).

most powerful weapons and machines, including firearms and big ships. But the Romans and other Christians decided not to tell the Arabs about the change; they would keep it a secret so as to surprise them. So the Arabs went to sleep, thinking that they knew the rules of the power game.

At this point, Chama would stop speaking and jump to her feet, in order to dramatize the story for Samir and me, all but ignoring Lalla Mani and Lalla Radia, who would be crying out in protest. Meanwhile, Aunt Habiba would be twisting her mouth, so that you would not see that she was smiling. Then Chama would raise up her white lace *qamis*, so as to liberate her legs and leap onto an empty sofa. She would stretch out in a sleeping position, bury her head in one of the huge cushions, push her rebellious red hair over her freckled face and declare, 'The Arabs are sleeping now.' Then she would close her eyes and start to snore, only to spring up a moment later, look around as if she had just come back from a very deep sleep, and fix her eyes on Samir and me as if she had never seen us before.

'The Arabs finally woke up a few weeks ago!' she would say. 'Harun al-Rashid's bones have become dust, and the dust has melted with the rain. The rain ran down to the Tigris River, and off to the sea where all big things become tiny, and get lost in the fury of the waves. A French king is now ruling in our part of the world. His title is Président de la République Française. He has a huge palace in Paris called the Élysée and he has, oh surprise, only one wife! No harem in sight. And that single wife spends her time running in the streets, with a short skirt, and a low neckline. Everybody can stare at her ass and bosom, but no one doubts for a moment that the president of the French Republic is the most powerful man in the country. Men's power is no longer measured by the number of women they can imprison. But this is news in Fez Medina, because the clocks are still frozen in Harun al-Rashid's time!'

Then Chama would jump back to the sofa, close her eyes, and bury her face in the flowered silk cushion again. Silence.

Samir and I loved Chama's story because she was such a good actress. I would always watch her closely to learn how to put movements into words. You had to use the words, and at the same time make the gestures with your body. But not everyone was as entranced with Chama's story as were Samir and I. Her own mother, Lalla Radia, was at first appalled, and then outraged, especially at the mention of Caliph Harun al-Rashid. Lalla Radia was a literate woman who read history books, a skill she had learned from her father, a famous religious authority in Rabat. She did not like people making light of caliphs in general, and Harun al-Rashid in particular. 'O Allah!' she would cry, 'Pardon my daughter, for she is attacking the caliphs again! And confusing the children! Two equally monstrous sins. Poor little ones, they will have such a distorted view of their ancestors, if Chama keeps this up.'

Lalla Radia would then ask Samir and me to sit near her so she could tell us the correct version of history, and make us love Caliph Harun. 'He was the prince of all caliphs,' she would say, 'the one who conquered Byzance and made the Muslim flag fly high in Christian capitals.' She also insisted that her daughter was all wrong about harems. Harems were wonderful things. All respectable men provided for their womenfolk, so that they did not have to go out into dangerous, unsafe streets. They gave them lovely palaces with marble floors and fountains, good food, nice clothes, and jewelry. What more did a woman need to be happy? It was only poor women like Luza, the wife of Ahmed the doorkeeper, who needed to go outside, to work and feed themselves. Privileged women were spared that trauma.

Samir and I often felt overwhelmed by all these contradictory opinions, and so we would try to organize the information a bit. Grownups were so untidy. A harem had to do with men and women – that was one fact. It also had to do with a house, walls and the streets – that was another fact. All of this was quite simple and easily to visualize: put four walls in the midst of the streets and you have a house. Then put the women in the house, and let the men go out: you have a harem. But what would happen, I ventured to ask Samir, if we put the men in the house, and let the women go out? Samir, said that I was complicating things, just at the moment when we were getting somewhere. So I agreed to put the women back in and the men back out, and we proceeded with our inquiry. The problem was that the walls and everything worked for our harem in Fez, but did not work at all for the harem on the farm.

6

Tamou's Horse

The harem on the farm was housed in a gigantic T-shaped one-story building surrounded by gardens and ponds. The right side of the house belonged to the women, the left to the men, and a delicate two-meter-high bamboo fence marked the *hudud* (the frontier) between them. The two sides of the house were in fact two similar buildings, built back to back, with symmetrical façades and roomy arched colonnades which kept the salons and smaller rooms cool, even when it was hot outside. The colonnades were perfect for playing hide-and-go-seek, and the children on the farm were much more daring than the ones in Fez. They would climb up the columns with their bare feet, and jump down like acrobats. They were also not afraid of the frogs, tiny lizards, and little flying animals that seemed to leap out at you non-stop whenever you crossed the corridors. The floors were paved with black and white tiles, and the columns were inlaid with a rare combination of pale yellow and dark gold mosaic that Grandfather liked, and that I have never seen elsewhere. The

51

gardens were surrounded by high delicate wrought-iron grilles with arched doors that always seemed closed, but we only had to push at them to get out into the fields. The men's garden had a few trees and a lot of neatly kept flowering shrubs, but the women's garden was another story altogether. It was overrun with strange trees and bizarre plants and animals of all kinds, because each co-wife claimed her own little plot of land which she declared to be her garden, where she raised vegetables, hens, ducks, and peacocks. You could not even take a walk in the women's garden without trespassing on someone's territory, and the animals would always follow you around, even under the arches of the paved colonnades, making a terrible racket which contrasted sharply with the monastery-like silence of the men's garden.

Besides the farm's main building, there were adjoining pavilions scattered about. Yasmina had the one on the right. She had insisted on it, explaining to Grandfather that she had to be as far away from Lalla Thor as possible. Lalla Thor had her own self-contained palace in the main building, with wall-to-wall mirrors and colorful woodwork on the ceilings, mirrors, and chandeliers. Yasmina's pavilion, on the other hand, consisted of a large, very simple room, with no luxuries. She did not care about all that, as long as she could stay away from the main building, and have enough space to experiment with trees and flowers, and raise all kinds of ducks and peacocks. Yasmina's pavilion also had a second floor, which had been built for Tamou after she fled the war in the Rif Mountains to the north. Yasmina took care of Tamou when she was sick, and the two became close friends.

Tamou came in 1926, after the defeat of Abdelkrim by the combined Spanish and French armies. She appeared early one morning over the horizon of the flat Gharb Plain, riding a Spanish saddled horse, and dressed in a man's white cape and a woman's headdress so that the soldiers would not shoot at her. All the co-wives loved to describe her arrival at the farm, and it was as good as the tales of the thousand and one nights, or even better, since Tamou was there to listen and smile and be the star. She had appeared that morning wearing heavy silver Berber bracelets with points sticking out, the kind of bracelets that you could use to defend yourself if necessary. She also had a *khandjar*, or dagger, dangling from her right hip and a real Spanish rifle that she kept hidden in her saddle, beneath her cape. She had a triangular-shaped face with a green tattoo on her pointed chin, piercing black eyes that looked at you without blinking, and a long, copper-colored braid that hung over her left shoulder. She stopped a few meters from the farm and asked to be received by the master of the house.

No one knew it that morning, but life on the farm was never going to be the same again. For Tamou was a Riffan and a war heroine. Morocco was full of admiration for the Rif people, the only ones who had kept on fighting the foreigners long after the rest of the country had given up, and here was this woman, clad as a warrior, crossing the ᶜArbaoua frontier into the French Zone all by herself to look for help. And because she was a war heroine, certain rules did not apply to her. She even behaved as though she did not know about tradition.

Grandfather probably fell in love with Tamou the first minute he saw her, but he did not realize it for months, so complex were the circumstances surrounding their meeting. Tamou had come to the farm with a mission. Her people were stranded in a guerrilla ambush in the Spanish Zone, and she needed to bring them aid. So Grandfather gave her the help she needed, first signing a quick marriage contract to justify her presence on the farm, in case the French police came looking for her. Then Tamou asked him to help her bring food and medicine to her people. There were many injured, and with the defeat of

Abdelkrim, each village had to survive on its own. Grandfather gave her the supplies and she left at night with two trucks, rolling slowly down the side of the road, with the lights out. Two peasants from the farm, posing as salesmen, rode on donkeys up ahead, scouting for trouble and signaling back to the trucks with torches.

When Tamou returned to Grandfather's farm a few days later, one of the trucks was loaded with corpses, covered with vegetables. They were the bodies of her father and husband, and her two little children, one boy and one girl. She stood silently by as the corpses were unloaded from the trucks. Then, the co-wives brought her a stool to sit on, and she just sat there watching as the men dug holes in the ground, placed the corpses inside, and covered them with the earth. She did not cry. The men planted flowers to camouflage the tombs. When they had finished, Tamou could not stand, and Grandfather called Yasmina, who took her arm and led her to her pavilion, where she put her to bed. For many months after that, Tamou did not talk, and everyone thought she had lost the capacity to speak.

Tamou screamed regularly in her sleep though, facing invisible attackers in her nightmares. The moment she closed her eyes, the war was on, and she would jump up onto her feet, or throw herself down on her knees, all the while begging for mercy in Spanish. She needed someone to help her through her grief without asking intrusive questions, or revealing anything to the Spanish and French soldiers reported to be making inquiries beyond the river. Yasmina was a person who could do this, and she took Tamou to her pavilion, where she cared for her for months, until she recovered. Then, one fine morning, Tamou was seen caressing a cat and putting a flower in her hair, and that night, Yasmina organized a party for her. The co-wives gathered together in her pavilion and sang so she would feel that she belonged. Tamou smiled a few times that night, and then she inquired about a horse she wished to ride the next day.

Tamou changed everything by her mere presence. Her own tiny body seemed to echo the same violent convulsions tearing her country apart, and she had frequent, wild urges to ride fast horses and do acrobatic stunts. They were her way of fighting her grief and finding a fleeting meaning in life. Instead of becoming jealous of her, Yasmina and all the other co-wives grew to admire her for, among other things, the many skills she had that women did not normally have. When Tamou became well, and started talking again, they discovered that she could shoot a gun, speak Spanish fluently, leap high in the air, somersault many times without getting dizzy, and even swear in many languages. Born into a mountain country constantly being crossed by foreign armies, she had grown up to confuse life with fighting, and relaxation with running. Her presence on the farm, with her tattoos, dagger, aggressive bracelets, and constant horseback riding, made the other women realize that there were many ways to be beautiful. Fighting, swearing, and ignoring tradition could make a woman irresistible. Tamou became a legend the moment she appeared. She made people aware of their inner force and their capacities to resist all kinds of fates.

During Tamou's illness, Grandfather had come to Yasmina's pavilion every day to inquire about her health. When she got better and requested a horse, however, he was very unsettled, for he feared she would run away. As thrilled as he was to see how fine she looked – so defiant and vibrant once again, with her copper braid, sharp black eyes, and green tatooed chin – he was not sure about her feelings for him. She was not really his wife. Their marriage had been just a legal arrangement, and she was a warrior after all, who might ride away at any moment and disappear into the Northern horizon. So he asked Yasmina to go with him for a walk in the fields, and he told her about his fears. Then Yasmina got very nervous, too, for she admired Tamou very much, and hated the idea of her leaving. So she suggested to Grandfather that he ask Tamou if she wanted to spend the night with him. 'If she says yes,' reasoned Yasmina, 'then she is not planning on leaving. If she says no, then she will.' Grandfather went back to the pavilion and talked with Tamou privately while Yasmina waited outside. But when he left, he was smiling, and Yasmina knew that Tamou had accepted his offer to become one of his co-wives. Months later, Grandfather built Tamou a new pavilion on top of Yasmina's and from then on, their two-story house outside of the main building became the official headquarters of both Tamou's horseback riding competitions and women's solidarity.

One of the first things that Yasmina and Tamou did, once the second pavilion was completed, was to grow a banana tree to make Yaya, the foreign black co-wife, feel at home. Yaya was the quietest of all the co-wives, a tall and lanky woman who looked terribly fragile in her yellow caftan. She had a thin-boned face with dreamy eyes, and changed turbans according to her moods, though her favorite color was yellow – 'like the sun. It gives you light.' She was prone to catching colds, spoke Arabic with an accent, and did not mix much with the other co-wives. Instead, she kept quietly to her room. Not long after her arrival, the other co-wives decided to do her share of housework, so fragile did she seem. In exchange, she promised to tell them a story once a week, describing life in her native village deep down in the South, in the land of the Sudan, the land of the blacks, where no orange or lemon trees grew, but where bananas and coconuts flourished. Yaya did not remember the name of her village, but that did not prevent her from becoming, like Aunt Habiba, the official storyteller of the harem. Grandfather helped her replenish her supply of tales by reading out loud passages from history books about the land of the Sudan, the kingdoms of Songhoy and Ghana, the golden gates of Timbuktu, and all the wonders of the forests down south which hid the sun. Yaya said that whites were common – they could be found anywhere in the four corners of the universe – but blacks were a special race because they existed only in the Sudan and neighboring lands, south of the Sahara Desert.

During storytelling night, all the co-wives would gather in Yaya's room, and tea trays would be brought in, while she talked about her wonderful homeland. After a few years, the co-wives knew the details of her life so well that they could fill in for her when she hesitated or started doubting the faithfulness of her memory. And one day, after listening to her describing her village, Tamou said. 'If all you need is a banana tree to feel at home on this farm, we'll grow you one right here.' At first, of course, no one believed that it would be possible to grow a banana tree in the Gharb, where the Northern winds blow down from Spain, and the heavy clouds roll in from the Atlantic Ocean.[1] But the most difficult task proved to be getting the tree. Tamou and Yasmina had to keep explaining what banana trees looked like to all the nomadic salesmen coming by on their donkeys, until finally someone brought them one from the Marrakech region. Yaya was so excited to see it that she took care of it as if it were a child, rushing to cover it with a large white sheet every time the cold wind blew. Years later, when the banana tree bore its first fruit, the co-wives organized a party and Yaya dressed in three layers of yellow caftans, put flowers around her turban, and danced away towards the river, giddy with happiness.

There were really no limits to what women could do on the farm. They could grow unusual plants, ride horses, and move

---

[1] This was in the 1940s. Now, thanks to modern technology, bananas and other equatorial fruits are being produced all over the Gharb Plain.

freely about, or so it seemed. In comparison, our harem in Fez was like a prison. Yasmina even said that the worst thing for a woman was to be cut off from nature. 'Nature is woman's best friend,' she often said. 'If you're having troubles, you just swim in the water, stretch out in a field, or look up at the stars. That's how a woman cures her fears.'

7

The Harem Within

Our harem in Fez was surrounded by high walls and, with the exception of the little square chunk of sky that you could see from the courtyard below, nature did not exist. Of course, if you rushed like an arrow up to the terrace, you could see that the sky was larger than the house, larger than everything, but from the courtyard, nature seemed irrelevant. It had been replaced by geometric and floral designs reproduced on tiles, woodwork, and stucco. The only strikingly beautiful flowers we had in the house were those of the colorful brocades which covered the sofas and those of the embroidered silk drapes that sheltered the doors and windows. You could not, for example, open a shutter to look outside when you wanted to escape. All the windows opened onto the courtyard. There were none facing the street.

Once a year, during springtime, we went on a *nzaha*, or picnic, at my uncle's farm in Oued Fez, ten kilometers from the city. The important adults rode in cars, while the children, divorced aunts, and other relatives were put into two big trucks rented for the occasion. Aunt Habiba and Chama always carried tambourines, and they would make such a hell of a noise along the way that the truck driver would go crazy. 'If you ladies don't stop this,' he would shout, 'I'm going to drive off the road and throw everyone into the valley.' But his threats always came to nothing, because his voice would be drowned out by the tambourines and hand clapping.

On picnic day, everyone woke up at dawn and buzzed around the courtyard as if it were a religious festival day with groups of people organizing food here, drinks there, and putting drapes and carpets into bundles everywhere. Chama and Mother took care of the swings. 'How can you have a picnic without swings?' they would argue whenever Father suggested they forget about them for once, because it took so much time to hang them from the trees. 'Besides,' he would add, just to provoke Mother, 'swings are fine for children, but when heavy grownups are involved, the poor trees might suffer.' While Father talked and waited for Mother to get angry, she would just keep on packing up the swings and the ropes to tie them with, without a single glance in his direction. Chama would sing aloud, 'If men can't tie the swings/women will do it/Lallallalla,' imitating the high-pitched melody of our national anthem 'Maghribuna watanuna' (Our Morocco, Our Homeland).[1] Meanwhile, Samir and I would be feverishly looking for our espadrilles, for there was no help to be had from our mothers, so involved were they in their own projects, and Lalla Mani would be counting the number of glasses and plates 'just to evaluate the damage, and see how many will be broken by the end of the day.' She could do without the picnic, she often said, especially since as far as tradition was

---

[1] Maghrib is the Arabic name for Morocco, the land of the setting sun, from *gharb* (west).

concerned, its origin was dubious. 'There's no record of it in the Hadith,' she said, 'It might even be counted as a sin on Judgment Day.'[2]

We would arrive on the farm in mid-morning, equipped with dozens of carpets and light sofas and *khanouns*.[3] Once the carpets had been unfolded, the light sofas would be spread out, the charcoal fires lit, and the shish kebabs grilled. The teakettles would sing along with the birds. Then, after lunch, some of the women would scatter into the woods and fields, searching for flowers, herbs, and other kinds of plants to use in their beauty treatments. Others would take turns on the swings. Only after sunset would we make the journey back to the house, and the gate would be closed behind us. And for days after that, Mother would feel miserable. 'When you spend a whole day among trees,' she would say, 'waking up with walls as horizons becomes unbearable.'

You could not get into our house, except by passing through the main gate controlled by Ahmed the doorkeeper. But you could get out a second way, by using the roof-level terrace. You could jump from our terrace to the neighbors' next door, and then go out to the street through their door. Officially, our terrace key was kept in Lalla Mani's possession, with Ahmed turning off the lights to the stairs after sunset. But because the terrace was constantly being used for all kinds of domestic activities throughout the day, from retrieving olives that were

---

[2] The Hadith is a compilation of the Prophet Mohammed's deeds and sayings. Recorded and written down after his death, the Hadith is considered to be one of the primary sources of Islam, the first being the Koran, the book revealed directly by Allah to his Prophet.

[3] *Khanouns* are portable charcoal fire containers, the Moroccan equivalent of the barbecue grill. They can be made of pottery or metal.

stored in big jars up there, to washing and drying clothes, the key was often left with Aunt Habiba, who lived in the room right next to the terrace.

The terrace exit route was seldom watched, for the simple reason that getting from it to the street was a difficult undertaking. You needed to be quite good at three skills: climbing, jumping, and agile landing. Most of the women could climb up and jump fairly well, but not many could land gracefully. So, from time to time, someone would come in with a bandaged ankle, and everyone would know just what she'd been up to. The first time I came down from the terrace with bleeding knees, Mother explained to me that a woman's chief problem in life was figuring out how to land. 'Whenever you are about to embark on an adventure,' she said, 'you have to think about the landing. Not about the takeoff. So whenever you feel like flying, think about how and where you'll end up.'

But there was also another, more solemn reason why women like Chama and Mother did not consider escaping from the terrace to be a viable alternative to using the front gate. The terrace route had a clandestine, covert dimension to it, which was repulsive to those who were fighting for the principle of a woman's right to free movement. Confronting Ahmed at the gate was a heroic act. Escaping from the terrace was not, and did not carry with it that inspiring, subversive flame of liberation.

None of this intrigue applied, of course, to Yasmina's farm. The gate had hardly any meaning, because there were no walls. And to be in a harem, I thought, you needed a barrier, a frontier. That summer, when I visited Yasmina, I told her what Chama had said about how harems got started. When I saw that she was listening, I decided to show off all my historical knowledge, and started talking about the Romans and their harems, and how the Arabs became the sultans of the planet thanks to Caliph Harun al-Rashid's one thousand women, and how the Christians tricked the Arabs by changing the rules on them while they were asleep. Yasmina laughed a lot when she heard the story, and said that she was too illiterate to evaluate the historical facts, but that it all sounded very funny and logical too. I then asked her if what Chama had said was true or false, and Yasmina said that I needed to relax about this right-and-wrong business. She said that there were things which could be both, and things which could be neither. 'Words are like onions,' she said. 'The more skins you peel off, the more meanings you encounter. And when you start discovering multiplicities of meanings, then right and wrong becomes irrelevant. All these questions about harems that you and Samir have been asking are all fine and good, but there will always be more to be discovered.' And then she added, 'I am going to peel one more skin for you now. But remember, it is only one among others.'

The word 'harem', she said, was a slight variation of the word *haram*, the forbidden, the proscribed. It was the opposite of *halal*, the permissible. Harem was the place where a man sheltered his family, his wife or wives, and children and relatives. It could be a house or a tent, and it referred both to the space and to the people who lived within it. One said 'Sidi So-and-So's harem', referring both to his family members and to his physical home. One thing that helped me see this more clearly was when Yasmina explained that Mecca, the holy city, was also called Haram. Mecca was a space where behavior was strictly codified. The moment you stepped inside, you were bound by many laws and regulations. People who entered Mecca had to be pure: they had to perform purification rituals, and refrain from lying, cheating, and doing harmful deeds. The city belonged to Allah and you had to obey his *shari'a*, or sacred law, if you entered his territory. The same thing applied to a harem when it was a house belonging to a man. No other men could enter it without the owner's permission, and when they did, they had to obey his rules. A harem was about private space and the rules regulating it. In addition, Yasmina said, it did not need walls. Once you knew what was forbidden, you carried the harem within. You had it in your head, 'inscribed under your forehead and under your skin'. That idea of an invisible harem, a law tattooed in the mind, was frightfully unsettling to me. I did not like it at all, and I wanted her to explain more.

The farm, said Yasmina, was a harem, although it did not have walls. 'You only need walls, if you have streets!' But if you decided, like Grandfather, to live in the countryside, then you didn't need gates, because you were in the middle of the fields and there were no passersby. Women could go freely out into the fields, because there were no strange men hovering around, peeping at them. Women could walk or ride for hours without seeing a soul. But if by chance they did meet a male peasant along the way, and he saw that they were unveiled, he would cover his head with the hood of his own *djellaba* to show that he was not looking. So in this case, Yasmina said, the harem was in the peasant's head, inscribed somewhere under his forehead. He knew that the women on the farm belonged to Grandfather Tazi, and that he had no right to look at them.

This business of going around with a frontier inside the head disturbed me, and discreetly I put my hand to my forehead to make sure it was smooth, just to see if by any chance I might be harem-free. But then, Yasmina's explanation got even more alarming, because the next thing she said was that any space you entered had its own invisible rules, and you needed to figure them out. 'And when I say space,' she continued, 'It can be any space – a courtyard, a terrace, or a room, or even the street for that matter. Wherever there are human beings, there is a *qaᵓida*, or invisible rule. If you stick to the *qaᵓida*, nothing bad can happen to you.' In Arabic, she reminded me, *qaᵓida* meant many different things, all of which shared the same basic premise. A mathematical law or a legal system was a *qa'ida*, and so was the foundation of a building. *Qa'ida* was also a custom, or a behavioral code. *Qa'ida* was everywhere. Then she added something which really scared me: 'Unfortunately, most of the time, the *qa'ida* is against women.'

'Why?' I asked. 'That's not fair, is it?' And I crept closer so as not to miss a word of her answer. The world, Yasmina said, was not concerned about being fair to women. Rules were made in such a manner as to deprive them in some way or another. For example, she said, both men and women worked from dawn until very late at night. But men made money and women did not. That was one of the invisible rules. And when a woman worked hard, and was not making money, she was stuck in a harem, even though she could not see its walls. 'Maybe the rules are ruthless because they are not made by women,' was Yasmina's final comment. 'But why aren't they made by women?' I asked. 'The moment women get smart and start asking that very question,' she replied, 'instead of dutifully cooking and washing dishes all the time, they will find a way to change the rules and turn the whole planet upside down.' 'How long will that take?' I asked, and Yasmina said, 'A long time.'

I asked her next if she could tell me how to figure out the invisible rule or *qa'ida*, whenever I stepped into a new space. Were there signals, or something tangible that I could look for? No, she said, unfortunately not, there were no clues, except for the violence after the fact. Because the moment I disobeyed an invisible rule, I would get hurt. However, she noted that many of the things people enjoyed doing most in life, like walking around, discovering the world, singing, dancing, and expressing an opinion, often turned up in the strictly forbidden category. In fact, the *qa'ida*, the invisible rule, often was much worse than walls and gates. With walls and gates, you at least knew what was expected from you.

At those words, I almost wished that all rules would suddenly materialize into frontiers and visible walls right before my very eyes. But then I had another uncomfortable thought. If Yasmina's farm was a harem, in spite of the fact that there were no walls to be seen, then what did *hurriya*, or freedom, mean? I shared this thought with her, and she seemed a little worried, and said that she wished I would play like other kids, and stop worrying about walls, rules, constraints, and the meaning of *hurriya*. 'You'll miss out on happiness if you think too much about walls and rules, my dear child,' she said. 'The ultimate goal of a woman's life is happiness. So don't spend your time looking for walls to bang your head on.' To make me laugh, Yasmina would spring up, run to the wall, and pretend to pound her head against it, screaming, '*Aie, aie!* The wall hurts! The wall is my enemy!' I exploded with laughter, relieved to learn that bliss was still within reach, in spite of it all. She looked at me and put her finger to her temple, 'You understand what I mean?'

Of course I understood what you meant, Yasmina, and happiness did seem absolutely possible, in spite of harems, both visible and invisible. I would run to hug her, and whisper in her ear as she held me and let me play with her pink pearls. 'I love you Yasmina. I really do. Do you think I will be a happy woman?'

'Of course you will be happy!' she would exclaim. 'You will be a modern, educated lady. You will realize the nationalists' dream. You will learn foreign languages, have a passport, devour books, and speak like a religious authority. At the very least, you will certainly be better off than your mother. Remember that even I, as illiterate and bound by tradition as I am, have managed to squeeze some happiness out of this damned life. That is why I don't want you to focus on the frontiers and the barriers all the time. I want you to concentrate on fun and laughter and happiness. That is a good project for an ambitious young lady.'

8

Aquatic Dishwashing

To reach Yasmina's farm we only had to travel a few hours, but it might as well have been one of Aunt Habiba's faraway islands in the China Sea. Women on the farm did things we'd never even heard of in the city, like fishing, tree climbing, and bathing in a stream that was rushing on to the Sebou River before heading to the Atlantic Ocean. The women even started participating in horseback riding competitions, after Tamou arrived from the North. Women had ridden horses on the farm before Tamou, but only discreetly, when the men were away, and they'd never really gone very far. Tamou turned riding into a solemn ritual, with fixed rules, and drills, and ostentatious awards ceremonies and prizes.

The winner of the race would receive a prize made by the last one to cross the finish line: an enormous *pastilla*, the most delicious of all of Allah's varied foods. At once a pastry and a meal, *pastilla* is sweet and salty, made of pigeon meat and nuts, sugar, and cinnamon. Oh! *Pastilla* crunches when you munch on it, and you have to eat it with delicate gestures, no rushing please, or else you will get sugar and cinnamon all over your face. *Pastilla* takes days to prepare because it is made of layers of sheer, almost transparent crust, stuffed with roasted and slightly crushed almonds, along with a lot of other surprises. Yasmina often said that if women were smart, they would sell the treat and make some money, instead of serving it as part of their banal housework duty.

With the exception of Lalla Thor, who was a city woman with very white, lifeless skin, most of the co-wives had the unmistakably rural features of mountainous Morocco. Also unlike Lalla Thor, who never did any housework and kept her three layers of caftans hanging leisurely down to her ankles, the co-wives tucked theirs into their belts, and hitched their sleeves up under their arms with colored elastics camouflaged to look like the traditional *takhmal*.[1] This style of dress allowed them to move swiftly throughout the day, performing household chores, and feeding people and animals.

One of the constant preoccupations of the co-wives was how to make housework more entertaining, and one day Mabrouka, who loved swimming, suggested that they try washing the dishes in the river. Lalla Thor was scandalized, and said that the idea was totally against Muslim civilization. 'These peasant women are going to destroy the reputation of this house,' she

---

[1] The word *takhmal* comes from the colloquial Arabic verb *khammal*, 'to engage in thorough cleaning duties.' The *takhmal* is a long embroidered ribbon or elastic band that women used for holding back long sleeves. They would take the one-meter-long ribbon, knot it so as to form a loop, and twist it into a figure eight. Then they would slip their arm into it, with the knot in the back, and tuck their sleeve into the ribbon, close to the armpit. To hide the practical aspect of the *takhmal*, many women embroidered the ribbon or the elastic band with pearls and beads; rich women used pearl necklaces or gold chains instead of ribbons or bands.

fumed, 'just as the venerable historian Ibn Khaldun predicted six hundred years ago in his *Muqaddimah*, when he said that Islam was essentially a city culture and peasants were its threat.[2] Having so many co-wives from the mountains was bound to lead to disaster.' Yasmina retorted that Lalla Thor would be much more useful to the Muslims if she stopped reading old books and started working like everyone else. But Lalla Thor took the matter to Grandfather, so jealous was she of the co-wives' attempt to have some fun, and he summoned Mabrouka and Yasmina to him. He asked them to explain their project. They did so, and then argued that although they were indeed both illiterate peasants, they were not dumb, and simply could not take Ibn Khaldun's words as sacred. After all, they said, he was just a historian. They would gladly renounce their proposed project, if Lalla Thor could produce a *fatwa* (decree) from the Qaraouiyine Mosque religious authorities banning women from washing dishes in rivers, but until that time, they would do as they pleased. After all, the river was Allah's creation, a manifestation of his power, and if, in any case, swimming were a sin, they would pay for it once in front of him, on Judgment Day. Grandfather, impressed by their logic, adjourned the meeting by saying that he was glad that responsi-

---

[2] One of Islam's most brilliant social historians, Ibn Khaldun lived in Muslim Spain and North Africa during the fourteenth century. In his masterpiece, the *Muqaddimah* (Introduction), he tried to submit history to a meticulous analysis so as to discover its guiding principles. In so doing, he identified city peoples as the positive poles of Muslim culture, and peripheral peoples, such as peasants and nomads, as the negative, destructive ones. This perception of urban centers as birthplaces of ideas, culture, and wealth, and rural populations as unproductive, rebellious, and undisciplined has infiltrated all Arab visions of development up until our own day. Even today in Morocco, the epithet *'aroubi*, that is, a person of rural origin, is still a commonly heard insult.

bility was an individual matter in Islam.

On the farm, as in all harems, household tasks were performed according to a strict rotation system. Women organized themselves into small teams formed along friendship and interest lines, and split the chores among them. The team that took care of the cooking one week would clean the floors the next, prepare tea and coffee and take care of the beverages the third, undertake the washing in the fourth, and relax and take a rest in the fifth. Rarely did all the women come together as a single group to perform one task. The exception was washing dishes, that usually tedious chore that was transformed after Mabrouka's suggestion (at least during the summer when I was there) into a fantastic aquatic show, complete with participants, spectators, and cheerleaders.

The women would stand in the river in two rows. In the first row, they stood, almost fully clad, in water up to their knees. In the second row, where only the women who swam well were allowed to stand, the water reached their waists and they were often half-clad in *qamis* only, tucked up high into tightened belts. Their heads would be uncovered too, because they could not fight the current while worrying about the possibility of losing scarves and turbans made of precious embroidered silks. The first row would undertake the initial cleaning, scouring the pots and pans and *tagines* (earthenware stewpots) with *tadekka*, a paste made of the sand and clay from the riverbanks. Then they would roll the pots and pans through the water to the second row for another cleaning. Meanwhile, the rest of the kitchenware would be circulating cross-current, from one hand to the next in a chain-like progression, with the water rinsing away the *tadekka*.

Finally, Mabrouka, the swimming star, would appear on the scene. Kidnapped from a village near the coastal city of Agadir during the civil war that ensued after the French took over, she had spent her childhood diving into the ocean from high cliffs.

Not only could she swim like a fish and stay under water for long periods of time, but she also rescued many of the co-wives from being swept away to Kenitra, the city where the Sebou River joins the sea. Her job during the dishwashing expeditions was to catch all the pots and pans that escaped the other co-wives' grasps, fight the current, and bring them back to shore. The women would clap and cheer whenever she emerged from the water, a pot or a pan on her head, and the 'criminal' who had let the pot slip by would have to grant her a wish that very night. The wish varied according to the skills of the culprit. Whenever Yasmina was at fault, Mabrouka asked for *sfinge*, Grandmother's incomparable doughnuts.

When the pots had been cleaned, they were sent back to Yasmina, who handed them to Krisha, the key man of the entire operation. Krisha, which literally means 'the Tummy,' was the nickname that the ladies had given to Mohammed al-Gharbaoui, their favorite and very spoiled driver. Krisha was a local Gharbaoui, born on the Gharb Plain by the sea between Tangier and Fez. He lived with his wife Zina a few hundred meters away from the farm, had never left his village, and did not feel that he was missing much. 'A more beautiful spot than Gharb, one cannot find in all the world,' he would say, 'with the exception of Mecca.' He was very tall and always wore an impressive white turban and a heavy brown *burnous* (cape) that he threw elegantly over his shoulders. In fact, he looked as though he should be a figure of authority, but somehow, he was not. He was not interested in exercising power or defending order. Enforcing the rules bored him. He was just a nice man who believed that most of Allah's creatures had enough brains to behave and act responsibly, starting with his wife who did very little housework and got away with it. 'If she does not like housework,' he would say, 'that's okay. I am not going to divorce her for that. We can manage.'

Krisha was not what you would call a busy man. When not driving his cart, he was either eating or sleeping, but he often got intensively involved in the women's activities, especially when they required the transportation of people or things.

Dishwashing in the river would have been impossible without Krisha. Many of the items to be washed were heavy brass pots, iron pans, and clay tagines which weighed well over six kilos each. (To feed everyone in a big household like the farm's, you needed large pots and pans.) Carrying them from the kitchens to the riverbank would have been impossible without the help of Krisha and his horse-drawn cart. Because Krisha, the Tummy, could not resist a good meal, you could get him to move mountains if you prepared his favourite couscous, with dried raisins, stuffed pigeons, and a lot of honeyed onions.

One of Krisha's official duties was to take the women to the *hammam*, or public baths, once every two weeks. The *hammam* was located in the neighboring village of Sidi Slimane, ten kilometers away from the farm, and riding with Krisha was always great fun. The women would keep jumping in and out of the cart, and ask every two minutes to stop 'so we can go pee.' He always had the same answer, which made everyone scream with laughter: 'Ladies, it is advisable, and even recommended, to pee in your *sarwal* (pantaloons). The most important thing is not whether you pee or not, but whether you stay in this damn cart until I arrive safely at Sidi Slimane.' When they arrived at Sidi Slimane, Krisha would climb down slowly from the driver's seat, stand on the pavement, and start counting the women on his fingers as they entered the *hammam*. 'Don't disappear in the steam, ladies, please' he would say, 'I need all of you to answer "present" when we return back tonight.'

Oh, they were wild on Yasmina's farm.

9

Moonlit Nights of Laughter

On Yasmina's farm, we never knew when we would eat. Sometimes, Yasmina only remembered at the last minute that she had to feed me, and then she would convince me that a few olives and a piece of her good bread, which she had baked at dawn, would be enough. But dining in our harem in Fez was an entirely different story. We ate at strictly set hours and never between meals.

To eat in Fez, we had to sit at our prescribed places at one of the four communal tables. The first table was for the men, the second for the important women, and the third for the children and less important women, which made us happy, because that meant that Aunt Habiba could eat with us. The last table was reserved for the domestics and anyone who had come in late, regardless of age, rank, or sex. That table was often overcrowded, and was the last chance to get anything to eat at all for those who had made the mistake of not being on time.

Eating at fixed hours was what Mother hated most about

communal life. She would nag Father constantly about the possibility of breaking loose and taking our immediate family to live apart. The nationalists advocated the end of seclusion and the veil, but they did not say a word about a couple's right to split off from their larger family. In fact, most of the leaders still lived with their parents. The male nationalist movement supported the liberation of women, but had not come to grips with the idea of the elderly living by themselves, nor with couples splitting off into separate households. Neither idea seemed right, or elegant.

Mother especially disliked the idea of a fixed lunch hour. She always was the last to wake up, and liked to have a late, lavish breakfast which she prepared herself with a lot of flamboyant defiance, beneath the disapproving stare of Grandmother Lalla Mani. She would make herself scrambled eggs and *baghrir*, or fine crêpes, topped with pure honey and fresh butter, and, of course, plenty of tea. She usually ate at exactly eleven, just as Lalla Mani was about to begin her purification ritual for the noon prayer. And after that, two hours later at the communal table, Mother was often absolutely unable to eat lunch. Sometimes, she would skip it altogether, especially when she wanted to annoy Father, because to skip a meal was considered terribly rude and too openly individualistic.

Mother dreamed of living alone with Father and us kids. 'Whoever heard of ten birds living together squashed into a single nest?' she would say. 'It is not natural to live in a large group, unless your objective is to make people feel miserable.' Although Father said that he was not really sure how the birds lived, he still sympathized with Mother, and felt torn between his duty towards the traditional family and his desire to make her happy. He felt guilty about breaking up the family solidarity, knowing only too well that big families in general, and harem life in particular, were fast becoming relics of the past. He even prophesied that in the next few decades, we would become like the Christians, who hardly ever visited their old parents. In fact, most of my uncles who had already broken away from the big house barely found the time to visit their mother, Lalla Mani, on Fridays after prayer anymore. 'Their kids do not kiss hands either,' ran the constant refrain. To make matters worse, until very recently, all my uncles had lived in our house, and had only split away when their wives' opposition to communal life had become unbearable. That is what gave Mother hope.

The first to leave the big family was Uncle Karim, Cousin Malika's father. His wife loved music and liked to sing while being accompanied by Uncle Karim, who played the lute beautifully. But he would rarely give in to his wife's desire to spend an evening singing in their salon, because his older brother Uncle ᶜAli thought it unbecoming for a man to sing or play a musical instrument. Finally, one day, Uncle Karim's wife just took her children and went back to her father's house, saying that she had no intention of living in the communal house ever again. Uncle Karim, a cheerful fellow who had himself often felt constrained by the discipline of harem life, saw an opportunity to leave and took it, excusing his actions by saying that he preferred to give in to his wife's wishes rather than forfeit his marriage. Not long after that, all my other uncles moved out, one after the other, until only Uncle ᶜAli and Father were left. So Father's departure would have meant the death of our large family. 'As long as [my] Mother lives,' he often said, 'I wouldn't betray the tradition.'

Yet Father loved his wife so much that he felt miserable about not giving in to her wishes and never stopped proposing compromises. One was to stock an entire cupboardful of food for her, in case she wanted to discreetly eat sometimes, apart from the rest of the family. For one of the problems in the communal house was that you could not just open a refrigerator when you were hungry and grab something to eat. In the first place, there were no refrigerators back then. More importantly, the entire idea behind the harem was that you lived according to the group's rhythm. You could not just eat when you felt like it. Lalla Radia, my uncle's wife, had the key to the pantry, and although she always asked after dinner what people wanted to eat the next day, you still had to eat whatever the group – after lengthy discussion – decided upon. If the group settled on couscous with chick-peas and raisins, then that is what you got. If you happened to hate chick-peas and raisins, you had no choice but to shut up and settle for a frugal dinner composed of a few olives and a great deal of discretion.

'What a waste of time,' Mother would say. 'These endless discussions about meals! Arabs would be much better off if they let each individual decide what he or she wanted to swallow. Forcing everyone to share three meals a day just complicates things. And for what sacred purpose? None of course.' From there, she would go on to say that her whole life was an absurdity, that nothing made sense, while Father would say that he could not just break away. If he did, tradition would vanish: 'We live in difficult times, the country is occupied by foreign armies, our culture is threatened. All we have left is these traditions.' This reasoning would drive Mother nuts: 'Do you think that by sticking together in this big, absurd house, we will gain the strength we need to throw the foreign armies out? And what is more important anyway, tradition or people's happiness?' That would put an abrupt end to the conversation. Father would try to caress her hand, but she would take it away. 'This tradition is choking me,' she would whisper, tears in her eyes.

So Father kept offering compromises. He not only arranged for Mother to have her own food stock, but also brought her things he knew she liked, such as dates, nuts, almonds, honey, flour, and fancy oils. She could make all the desserts and cookies she wanted, but she was not supposed to prepare a meat dish or a major meal. That would have meant the beginning of the end of the communal arrangement. Her flamboyantly prepared individual breakfasts were enough of a slap in the face to the rest of the family. Every once in a long while, Mother *did* get away with preparing a complete lunch or a dinner, but she had to not only be discreet about it but also give it some sort of exotic overtone. Her most common ploy was to camouflage the meal as a nighttime picnic on the terrace.

These occasional tête-à-tête dinners on the terrace during moonlit summer nights were another peace offering that Father made to help satisfy Mother's yearning for privacy. We would be transplanted to the terrace, like nomads, with mattresses, tables, trays, and my little brother's cradle, which would be set down right in the middle of everything. Mother would be absolutely out of her mind with joy. No one else from the courtyard dared to show up, because they understood all too well that Mother was fleeing from the crowd. What she most enjoyed was trying to get Father to depart from his conventional self-controlled pose. Before long, she would start acting foolishly, like a young girl, and soon, Father would chase her all around the terrace, when she challenged him. 'You can't run anymore, you have grown too old! All you're good for now is to sit and watch your son's cradle.' Father, who had been smiling up to that point, would look at her at first as if what she had just said had not affected him at all. But then his smile would vanish, and he would start chasing her all over the terrace, jumping over tea-trays and sofas. Sometimes both of them made up games which included my sister and Samir (who was the only one of the rest of the family allowed to attend our moonlit gatherings) and myself. More often, they completely forgot about the rest of the world, and we children would be sneezing all the next day because they had forgotten to put blankets on us when we had gone to sleep that night.

After these blissful evenings, Mother would be in an unusually

soft and quiet mood for a whole week. Then she would tell me
that whatever else I did with my life, I had to take her revenge. 'I
want my daughters' lives to be exciting,' she would say, 'very
exciting and filled with one hundred percent happiness, nothing
more, nothing less.' I would raise my head, look at her earnestly,
and ask what one hundred percent happiness meant, because I
wanted her to know that I intended to do my best to achieve it.
Happiness, she would explain, was when a person felt good,
light, creative, content, loving and loved, and free. An unhappy
person felt as if there were barriers crushing her desires and the
talents she had inside. A happy woman was one who could
exercise all kinds of rights, from the right to move to the right to
create, compete, and challenge, and at the same time could feel
loved for doing so. Part of happiness was to be loved by a man
who enjoyed your strength and was proud of your talents.
Happiness was also about the right to privacy, the right to retreat
from the company of others and plunge into contemplative
solitude. Or to sit by yourself doing nothing for a whole day,
and not give excuses or feel guilty about it either. Happiness was
to be with loved ones, and yet still feel that you existed as a
separate being, that you were not there just to make them happy.
Happiness was when there was a balance between what you gave
and what you took. I then asked her how much happiness she
had in her life, just to get an idea, and she said that it varied
according to the days. Some days she had only five percent;
others, like the evenings we spent with Father on the terrace, she
had full-blown one hundred percent happiness.

Aiming at one hundred percent happiness seemed a bit overwhelming to me, as a young girl, especially since I could see how
much Mother labored to sculpt her moments of happiness. How
much time and energy she put into creating those wonderful
moonlit evenings sitting close to Father, talking softly in his ear,
her head on his shoulder! It seemed quite an accomplishment to

me because she had to start working on him days ahead of time, and then she had to take care of all the logistics, like the cooking and the moving of the furniture. To invest so much stubborn effort just to achieve a few hours of happiness was impressive, and at least I knew it could be done. But how, I wondered, was I going to create such a high level of excitement for an entire lifetime? Well, if Mother thought it was possible, I should certainly give it a try.

'Times are going to get better for women now, my daughter,' she would say to me. 'You and your sister will get a good education, and you'll walk freely in the streets and discover the world. I want you to become independent, independent and happy. I want you to shine like moons. I want your lives to be a cascade of serene delights. One hundred percent happiness. Nothing more, nothing less.' But when I asked her for more details about how to create that happiness, Mother would grow very impatient. 'You have to work at it. One develops the muscles for happiness, just like for walking and breathing.'

So every morning, I would sit on our threshold, contemplating the deserted courtyard and dreaming about my beautiful future, a cascade of serene delights. Hanging on to the romantic moonlit terrace evenings, challenging your beloved man to forget about his social duties, relax and act foolish and gaze at the stars while holding your hand, I thought, could be one way to go about developing muscles for happiness. Sculpting soft nights, when the sound of laughter blends with the spring breezes, could be another.

But those magical evenings were rare, or so they seemed. During the days, life took a much more rigid and disciplined turn. Officially, there was no jumping around or foolishness allowed in the Mernissi household – all that was confined to clandestine times and spaces, such as late afternoons in the courtyard when the men were out, or evenings on the deserted terraces.

10

The Men's Salon

The problem with entertainment, fun, and foolishness at our house was that they could easily be missed. They were never planned in advance unless Cousin Chama or Aunt Habiba were in charge, and even then, they were subject to serious space constraints. Aunt Habiba's story-telling and Chama's theater plays had to take place upstairs. You could never really have fun for long in the courtyard; it was too public. Just as you were starting to have a good time, the men would come in with their own projects, which often involved a great deal of discussion, such as going over business matters, or listening to the radio and debating the news, or card playing, and then you would have to move elsewhere. Good entertainment needs concentration and silence in order for the masters of ceremony, the storytellers and the actors to create their magic. You could not create magic in the courtyard, where dozens of people were constantly crossing from one salon to the other, popping in and out of the corner staircases, or talking back and forth to one another from one floor to the next. And you certainly could not create magic when the men were talking politics, that is, listening to the radio on the loudspeakers, or reading the local and international press.

The men's political discussions were always highly emotionally charged. If you listened carefully to what they were saying, you had the impression that the world was coming to an end. (Mother said that if you believed the radio and the men's comments, the planet would have disappeared a long time ago.) They talked about the Allemane, or Germans, a new breed of Christians who were giving a beating to the French and the British, and they talked about a bomb that the Americans across the sea had dropped on Japan, which was one of the Asian nations near China, thousands of kilometers east of Mecca. Not only had the bomb killed thousands and thousands of people and melted their bodies, it had shaved entire forests off the face of the earth as well. The news about that bomb plunged Father, Uncle ᶜAli, and my young cousins into deep despair, for if the Christians had thrown that bomb on the Asians who lived so far away, it was only a matter of time before they attacked the Arabs. 'Sooner or later,' Father said, 'they will be tempted to burn the Arabs too.'

Samir and I loved the men's political discussions, because then we were allowed into the crowded men's salon, where Uncle and Father, each dressed comfortably in a white *djellabas*, sat surrounded by the *chabab*, or the youth – that is, the dozen adolescent and unmarried young men who lived in the house. Father often joked with the *chabab* about their uncomfortable, tight Western dress, and said that now they would have to sit on chairs. But of course everyone hated chairs; sofas were much more comfortable.

I would climb up into my father's lap and Samir would climb up into Uncle's. Uncle would be sitting cross-legged in the middle of the highest sofa, wearing his spotless white *djellabas* and a white turban, with his son Samir perched on his lap in Prince of Wales shorts. I would nestle in my father's lap, neatly dressed in one of my very short French white dresses with satin ribbons at the waist. Mother always insisted on dressing me in the latest Western fashions – short, fluffy lace dresses with colored ribbons and shiny black shoes. The only problem was that she would fly into a fury if I dirtied the dress, or disarranged the ribbons, and so I would often beg her to let me wear my comfortable little *sarwal* (harem pants), or any traditional outfit, which required less attention. But only on religious festival days, when Father insisted, would she let me wear my caftan, so anxious was she to see me escape tradition. 'Dress says so much about a woman's designs,' she said. 'If you plan to be modern, express it through what you wear, otherwise they will shove you behind the gates. Caftans may be of unparalleled beauty, but Western dress is about salaried work.' I therefore grew to associate caftans with lavish holidays, religious festivals, and the splendors of our ancestral past, and Western dress with pragmatic calculations and stern, professional, daily chores.

In the men's salon, Father always sat opposite Uncle, on the sofa near the radio, so he could control the dials. Each man would be dressed in a double *djellabas* – the outer one made of sheer snow-white pure wool, a specialty of Ouazzane, a religious city to the north with a fine weaving tradition; the inner one made of heavier cloth. Father would also wear his one little eccentricity, a pale yellow turban made of embroidered cotton from Cham (Syria).

'But what good does our wearing traditional dress do,' Father joked one day to my young cousins sitting around him, 'when all you young people dress like Rudolph Valentino?' Without exception, they all wore Western attire, and with their short hair uncovered and cut above the ears, they looked very much like the French soldiers standing at the end of the street. 'One day, we will probably manage to throw the French out, only to wake up and find out that we all look like them,' added Uncle.

Among the young cousins who frequented the salon were Samir's three brothers, Zin, Jawad, and Chakib, and all the sons of the widowed and divorced aunts and relatives who lived with us. Most of them went to the nationalist schools, but a few of the brightest attended the very select Collège Musulman, located just a few meters from our house. The Collège was a French secondary school which prepared the sons of prominent families to fill key positions, and the students' scholastic excellence was measured according to the degree to which they mastered both Arabic and French language and history. To beat the West, Arab youth needed mastery of at least two cultures.

Of all my male cousins, Zin was considered to be by far the most gifted. When in the salon, he would usually sit near Uncle, with the French papers ostentatiously displayed on his lap. He was extremely handsome with fine brown hair, almond-shaped eyes, high cheekbones, and a light mustache. He bore a distinct resemblance to Rudolf Valentino, whom we often saw on the screen at the Boujeloud Cinema, where we were treated to two films at a time, one Egyptian and in Arabic, and the other foreign and in French. The first time Samir and I saw Rudolf Valentino, we promptly adopted him as a member of our harem because he looked so much like our cousin Zin. By that time, Zin had already cultivated 'the Sheikh's' sullen expression, somber attire, parted hair, and tiny red flower in the breast pocket.

Appropriately, Zin's name meant 'beauty', and I admired his handsomeness and elegance. Like everyone else, I respected him for his eloquence in French, a language which no one else in the family had mastered at that point. I could listen to him uttering those bizarre French sounds for hours. Everybody else would stare at him in awe, too, whenever Uncle gestured to him to begin reading the French papers. He would start by quickly reading the headlines and then go back to the articles that Uncle or Father had picked out more or less intuitively, since their French was quite poor. These he would read out loud, before giving summaries in Arabic.

The way Zin spoke French, and most particularly, the way he rolled his *r*'s gave me thrills. My *r*'s were disastrously flat even in Arabic, and my teacher, Lalla Tam, would often stop me in my chanting of the Koran to remind me that my ancestors had had very forceful *r*'s. 'You have to respect your ancestors, Fatima Mernissi,' she would say, 'Why massacre the innocent alphabet?' I would stop, listen to her politely, and swear that I would respect my ancestors. Then I would gather all my thoracic strength and make a brave, desperate attempt to pronounce a robust *r*, only to end up choking. And here was talented Zin, so gifted and eloquent that he could speak French and roll hundreds of *r*'s without any apparent effort. Often I would stare at him intently, thinking that if I could just concentrate hard enough, some of his grace, and maybe his mysterious ability to roll *r*'s, would rub off on me.

Zin worked very hard at becoming the ideal modern nationalist, that is, one who possessed a vast knowledge of Arab history, legends, and poetry, as well as fluency in French, the language of our enemy, in order to decode the Christian press and uncover their plans. He succeeded beautifully. Although the modern Christians' supremacy in science and mathematics was evident, the nationalist leaders encouraged the youth to read the classic treaties of Avicenna and Al-Khwarizmi,[1] 'just to have an idea

---

[1] Avicenna (A.D. 980–1037), known in Arabic as Ibn Sina, and Al-Khwarizmi (circa A.D. 800–847) were two of the illustrious scholars of a brilliant intellectual and scientific Muslim community which started flourishing very early under the Abbasid Dynasty thanks to state financial support. Al-Ma^cmud (A.D. 813–833), the seventh caliph, was such an

about the way their minds functioned. It always helps to know that your ancestors were fast and precise.' Father and Uncle respected Zin as one of the new generation of Moroccans who was going to save the country. He led the procession to the Qaraouiyine Mosque on Fridays, when all the men of Fez, young and old, turned up in the traditional white *djellaba* and fine yellow leather slippers to go to public prayer.

Ostensibly, the reason for the Friday noon gathering at the mosque was religious, but everyone, including the French, knew that many important political decisions of the *Majlis al-Baladi*, or City Council, were in fact settled right there. Not only did all the members of the Council, like Uncle ʿAli, attend that prayer service, but delegates from all the city's interest groups, from the most prestigious to the most humble, were present as well. The mosque, which was open to everyone, compensated for the exclusive nature of the Council, which had been set up by the French, according to Uncle ʿAli, as an assembly of dignitaries. 'Although the French have dethroned their nobles and kings,' he said, 'they still prefer to talk with men of rank alone, and it is up to us, the locals, to be responsible and communicate with the people. Any person who holds a political office ought to attend the Friday prayer regularly. That's how you stay in touch with your constituency.'

Five groups who had insured the city's intellectual and economic position in Morocco for centuries were always heavily represented in the mosque on Fridays. First came the *ulema*, or men of learning, who devoted their lives to science, and could

example of a statesman who made it public policy to support the sciences. Avicenna's extensive writings enumerated all the medical knowledge of his day. Al-Khwarizmi pioneered the use of Hindu numbers and calculation techniques in Arab mathematics. These and other Arab scholars ultimately preserved and transmitted to the West a great body of knowledge founded upon the classical Greek, Persian, Sanskrit, and Syriac.

often trace their ancestry back to Andalusia or Muslim Spain. They kept the veneration of books and the book industry alive, from papermaking, calligraphy, and bookbinding, to encouraging reading, writing, and collecting rare editions. Then came the *sharifs*, or descendants of the Prophet, who enjoyed enormous prestige and played key symbolical roles during marriage, birth, and death rituals. The *sharifs* were known to be of modest means; making money and building fortunes were not their chief concerns. Those were the obsession of the *tujjar*, or merchants, who constituted the third, highly mobile and crafty group. They were the adventurers, and in the break between prayers, they would often describe their risky travels to Europe and Asia, where they bought luxury goods and machinery, or to the South, beyond the Sahara Desert.

Then came the *fellah* families, or landowners, the group to which Uncle and Father belonged. The word *fellah* meant two contradictory things: poor, landless peasants on the one hand, and rich landowners and sophisticated agricultural developers on the other. Uncle and Father were proud to be *fellah*, but they belonged to the second category. Uncle and Father were attached to their land, and nothing gave them more pleasure than spending long days on their farms even though they had chosen to live in the city. The *fellah* did their farming on a more or less large scale, and often were busy catching up on the modern agricultural techniques introduced by the colonial French. Many of the landowning families were like ours, originally from the pre-Rif Mountains north of the city, and were proud of their rural origins, especially when faced with the conceited arrogance of the Andalusians, the learned group. 'The *ulema* are important indeed,' said Father whenever the topic of the city's hierarchy came up, 'but if they did not have us to produce food for them, they would die of hunger. You can do a lot of things with a book – namely, look at it, read it, ponder its ideas, and so on. But you cannot eat it. That's the intellectual's problem. So one shouldn't be excessively impressed by an intellectual. It's better to be a *fellah* like us, who love the land and admire it, and then educate ourselves. If you can work the land and read the books, you can never go wrong.' Father worried a lot about the *chabab*, or family youth, getting too much pleasure from books and losing interest in the land, which was why he insisted that they stay with him on Uncle's farm, a few kilometers from Fez, during their summer holidays.

The fifth and largest key group in the city was that of the craftsmen, who had produced practically everything that was needed in Morocco before the French had invaded the markets with their machine-made goods. Districts in Fez were named after the products that the craftsmen produced there. Haddadin, literally, 'iron workers,' was the district where metal products were made from iron and brass. Debbaghin (treated leather) was the leather district; the potters worked in the Fakharin (pottery district); and you went to the Najjarine (wood district) to buy products made of wood. The most prosperous craftsmen were those who worked with gold and silver, and those who turned silk threads into luxurious *sfifa* (passementerie), to complement caftans pre-embroidered by women.[2] People from the same district often sat together in the mosque and went back home in a group, chatting and exchanging ideas about the latest news.

Cousin Zin and the other young men always walked to the

[2] Men and women complemented each other's work in the production process. For example, silk caftans would first be designed by a woman who would decide on the fabric and shape, and then would embroider it herself before giving it to a craftsman who would sew it and add the passementerie to the edges. The same happened with leather slippers: men would cut the leather to size, send the pieces to the women to be embroidered, and then the women would send them back to the men to be sewn.

Friday gatherings at the mosque on foot, while the older men followed just a few meters behind, sometimes on foot, and sometimes riding their mules. Samir and I loved it when Uncle and Father took their mules because then we could be part of the party too. We each would sit on our father's mule, in front of the saddle. Father hesitated about taking me to the mosque with him the first time, but I screamed so loudly that Uncle told him that there was nothing wrong with taking a little girl to the mosque. The Hadith reported that the Prophet, Allah's Prayer and Peace Upon Him, had conducted prayers in the mosque with a female child playing in front of him.

The only concession to tradition that the young men made in their Friday dress was that instead of keeping their heads uncovered, they wore the triangular felt cap that had become popular among the Egyptian nationalists. These felt caps could bring on trouble in times of agitation, when the French police got hysterical, because the cap fad had first swept our Medina after Allal al-Fassi, an often-imprisoned and exiled Fez-born hero who opposed the French presence in North Africa, appeared wearing one at the Qaraouiyine Mosque. Later, when our King Mohammed V wore the felt cap, elegantly sloping back from his serene forehead, at an official meeting with the French Résident Général in Rabat, foreign analysts of Arab affairs concluded that nothing good, as far as their interests were concerned, could be expected from him anymore. Any king who discarded his traditional turban in favor of a subversive felt hat could no longer be trusted.

In any case, tradition and modernity existed harmoniously side by side, both in the young men's dress and in our house during the men's news sessions. First, everyone would listen to the radio news in both Arabic and French. Then Father would turn off the radio, and the group would listen to the young men reading and commenting on the written press. Tea would be served, and

Samir and I were expected to listen without too much interruption. However, I would often press my head against Father's shoulder and whisper, 'Who are the Allemane (Germans)? Where did they come from, and why are they beating up the French? Where are they hiding, if the Spaniards are in the North and the French in the South?' Father always promised to explain it all to me later when we were by ourselves in our salon. And he did explain it many times, but I never got over my confusion, and neither did Samir, in spite of all our efforts to put the pieces of the puzzle together.

11

World War II:
View from the Courtyard

The Allemane (Germans) were Christians, that was for sure. They lived in the North like all the others, in what we call Blad Teldj, or the Snowland. Allah did not favor the Christians: their climate was harsh and cold, and that made them moody and, when the sun did not show up for months, nasty. To warm themselves up, they had to drink wine and other strong beverages, and then they got aggressive and started looking for trouble. They did drink tea sometimes though, just like everyone else, but even their tea was bitter and scalding and not at all like ours, which was always perfumed with mint or even absinthe or myrtle. Cousin Zin, who had visited England, said that the tea up there was so bitter, they mixed it with milk. So Samir and I poured some milk in our mint tea once, just to give it a try, and it was ugh! awful! No wonder the Christians were always miserable and looking for fights.

Anyway, it seemed that the Allemane, the Germans, had been preparing a huge and secret army for a long time. No one knew about it, and then one day, they invaded France. They colonized Paris, the French capital, and started giving people orders, just as the French were doing to us in Fez. We were lucky though, because at least the French did not like our Medina, the city of our ancestors, and had built the Ville Nouvelle for themselves. I asked Samir what would have happened if the French had liked the Medina, and he said that they would have thrown us right out, and taken our houses.

The mysterious Allemane were not only after the French, however; they had also declared war on the Jews. The Allemane forced the Jews to wear something yellow whenever they stepped out into the streets, just as the Muslim men asked the women to wear a veil, so they could be spotted immediately. Why the Allemane were after Jews, no one in the courtyard was ever really able to say. Samir and I kept asking questions, running around from one embroidery team to another on quiet afternoons, but all we got was speculation. 'It could be the same thing as with women here,' said Mother. 'No one really knows why men force us to wear veils. Something to do with the difference maybe. Fear of the difference makes people behave in very strange ways. The Allemane must feel safer when they are by themselves, just like the men in the Medina who get nervous whenever women appear. If the Jews insist on their difference, that could unsettle the Allemane. Crazy world.'

In Fez, the Jews had their own district, called the Mellah. It took exactly half an hour to get there from our house, and the Jews looked just like everyone else, dressing in long robes similar to our *djellabas*. They wore hats instead of turbans, that's all. They minded their own business and kept to their Mellah, making beautiful jewelry and pickling their vegetables in a most delicious way. Mother had tried to pickle zucchini, small cucumbers, and tiny eggplants the Mellah way, but she had never succeeded. 'They must say some magic words,' she concluded.

Like us, the Jews had their own prayers, loved their God, and taught His book to their children. They had built a synagogue for Him, which was like our mosque, and we shared the same prophets, with the exception of our beloved Mohammed, Allah's Prayer and Peace Upon Him. (I never went too far in listing the prophets, because it got complicated and I was afraid of making a mistake. My teacher Lalla Tam said that making mistakes in religious matters could send a person to hell. It was called *tashif*, or blasphemy, and as I already had decided that I was going to paradise, I tried to stay away from mistakes.) One thing was for sure, the Jews had always lived with Arabs, since the beginning of time, and the Prophet Mohammed had liked them when he first started preaching Islam. But then they did something nasty, and he decided, that if the two religions were to co-exist in the same city, they would have to live in separate quarters. Jews were well organized and had a strong sense of community, much stronger than ours. In the Mellah, the poor were always taken care of and all the children went to highly disciplined Alliance Israélite schools.

What I could not understand was, what were the Jews doing in the country of the Allemane? How did they get there, into Snowland? I thought that Jews, like Arabs, preferred warm climates and steered away from snow. They had lived in the city of Medina, in the middle of the Arabian Desert, during the Prophet's time, fourteen centuries ago, right? And before that, they had lived in Egypt, not that far from Mecca, and in Syria. At any rate, the Jews had always hung around with the Arabs.[1]

---

[1] This idea of Jews and Muslims belonging together may seem strange today, but the events in this book took place before the creation of the State of Israel in May 1948. At that time, this vision of a strong cultural and historical bond between Jews and Muslims was very prevalent, especially in Morocco, where both communities still had a fresh memory of the

During the Arab conquest of Spain, when the Arab Omayyad Dynasty of Damascus turned Andalusia into a shady garden, and built palaces in Cordoba and Seville, the Jews went right alongside. Lalla Tam had told us all about that, although she had talked so much about it that I had gotten confused, and thought it was mentioned in the Koran, our holy book.

For you see, most of the time, Lalla Tam did not bother to explain what the verses of the Koran meant. Instead, we copied them down into our *luha*, or tablet, on Thursdays, and learned them by heart on Saturdays, Sundays, Mondays, and Tuesdays. Each one of us would sit on our cushion, hold our *luha* on our lap, and read out loud, chanting back and forth until the words sank into our heads. Then on Wednesdays, Lalla Tam would make us recite what we had learned. You had to put your *luha* on your lap, face down, and recite the verses from memory. If you did not make any mistakes, Lalla Tam would smile. But she rarely smiled when it was my turn. 'Fatima Mernissi,' she would

Spanish Inquisition, which had led to their expulsion from Spain in 1492. Bernard Lewis wrote an interesting chapter about this pre-1948 vision, in which he explains that many Europeans then believed that the Jews and Muslims had conspired together against Christian interests in the nineteenth and early twentieth centuries (Bernard Lewis, 'Les Juifs pro-Islamiques,' in *Le retour de l'Islam*, French translation; Paris: Editions Gallimard, 1985, p. 315). The radical shift in perception regarding the alliances between the three religions around the Mediterranean has happened in an incredibly short time. In fact, even at the end of the 1940s, the Moroccan Jewish community was impressive in numbers and one of the pillars of tradition in North Africa, with deep roots reaching far back into the local Berber pre-Islamic culture. Since then, most Jews have left Morocco, migrating to Israel and other countries such as France and, later, Canada. Today, the Fez Mellah is entirely populated by Muslims, and the Jews left in the country number only in the hundreds. Therefore, many Moroccan Jewish intellectuals have been trying as fast as they can to document the cultural characteristics of the Moroccan Jewish community, one of the most ancient of the world, which has vanished in less than a decade.

say, her whip hovering above my head, 'you will not go far in life, if words keep going in one ear and out the other.' After recitation day, Thursday and Friday practically felt like holidays, although we did have to clean off the *luha* and write the new verses. But during all this time, Lalla Tam did not explain the verse. She said that it would be useless to do so. 'Just learn by heart what you have written on your *luha*,' she would say. 'No one will ask you your opinion.'

Still, she went on and on about our conquest of Spain, and when I got confused and believed it to be part of the holy book, she screamed that I was speaking utter blasphemy and summoned Father. It took him a long time to clear things up. He said that it was essential for a young lady who wanted to dazzle the Muslim world to know a few key dates, and then all the rest would fall nicely into place. Then he told me that the revelation of the Koran ended with the death of the Prophet, in the year 11 of the Hejira (Mohammed's exodus from Mecca), which is the year 632 in the Christian calendar. I asked Father to please simplify things for me by sticking to the Muslim calendar for the time being, because the Christian one was so confusing, but he said that a smart lady born on the shores of the Mediterranean Sea needed to be able to navigate two or three calendars at least. 'Switching calendars will become automatic if you start early enough,' he said. He did agree to skip mention of the Jewish calendar, though, because it was so much older than everyone else's, it made me dizzy just imagining how far back in time it went.

Anyway, to get back to the point, the Arabs conquered Spain almost one century after the Prophet's death, in the year 91 of the Hejira. Therefore, the conquest is not mentioned anywhere in the holy book. 'So, why does Lalla Tam keep talking about it?' I asked. Father said that that was probably because her family had come from Spain. Her last name was Sabata, a derivation of

Zapata, and her father still had the key to their house in Seville. 'She is just homesick,' Father said. 'Queen Isabella massacred most of her family.'

He went on the explain that the Jews and the Arabs had lived in Andalusia for seven hundred years, from the second to the eighth centuries of the Hejira (A.D. eighth to fifteenth centuries). Both peoples had gone to Spain when the Omayyad Dynasty had conquered the Christians and established an empire with Cordoba as its capital. Or was Granada the capital? Or was it Seville? Lalla Tam never mentioned one city without mentioning the others, so maybe the people had a choice among the three capitals, although normally, you were not allowed more than one. But nothing was normal about Spain, which the Omayyad re-named Al-Andalous.

The Omayyad caliphs were a merry bunch who had a lot of fun building a fabulous palace, the Alhambra, and tower, the Giralda. Then, wanting to show off to the rest of the world how enormous their empire was, they built an identical tower in Marrakech, and named it the Koutoubiya. As far as they were concerned, there was no frontier between Europe and Africa. 'Everyone is fond of mixing the two continents up,' said Father. 'Otherwise, why are the French camping right outside our door at this very moment?'

So the Arabs and the Jews lounged around up there in Andalusia for seven hundred years, enjoying themselves as they recited poetry and looked up at the stars from the middle of their lovely jasmine and orange gardens, which they watered through an innovative and complicated irrigation system. We forgot all about them down here in Fez until one day, the city woke up to see hundreds of them streaming down into Morocco, screaming with fright, their house keys in their hand. A ferocious Christian queen named Isabella the Catholic had emerged from the snow and was after them. She had given them one hell of a beating and

said, 'Either you pray like us, or we'll throw you into the sea.'
But in fact, she never gave them time to answer, and her soldiers
pushed everyone into the Mediterranean. Muslims and Jews
together swam to Tangier and Ceuta (unless they were among
the lucky ones who found boats) and then ran to Fez to hide.
That had happened five hundred years ago, and that was why we
had a huge Andalusian community right in the heart of the
Medina, near the Quaraouiyine Mosque, and the big Mellah, or
Jewish quarter, a few hundred meters away.

But that still does not explain how the Jews ended up in the
land of the Allemane, does it? Samir and I talked about this and
decided that maybe, when Isabella the Catholic started screaming, some of the Jews walked the wrong way, heading north
instead of south, and found themselves in the heart of Snowland.
Then, since the Allemane were Christians, like Isabella the
Catholic, they chased the Jews away because they did not pray
alike. But Aunt Habiba said that this explanation did not sound
right, because the Allemane were also fighting the French, who
were Christians too and worshipped the same God. So that put
an end to that theory. Religion could not explain the war going
on in Christendom.

I was about to suggest to Samir that we let the mysterious
Jewish question sit until the following year, when we would be
much older and wiser, when Cousin Malika came up with a
sensible but terrifying explanation. The war had to do with hair
color! The blond-haired tribes were fighting the brown-haired
people! Crazy! The Allemane, in this case, were the blonds, tall
and pale, while the French were the brunettes, smaller and
darker. The poor Jews, who had simply gone the wrong way
when Isabella chased everyone from Spain, were trapped
between the two. They just happened to be in the war zone, and
they just happened to have brown hair. They were not part of
any camp!

So, the mighty Allemane were after anyone with dark hair and dark eyes. Samir and I were terrified. We checked what Malika had said with Cousin Zin, and he said that she was absolutely right. Hi-Hitler — that was the name of the king of the Allemane — hated dark hair and dark eyes and was throwing bombs from planes wherever a dark-haired population was spotted. Jumping into the water would not do any good either, because he would send submarines to fish you out. Looking up at his older brother, Samir put his hands over his sleek jet-black hair, as if to hide it, and said, 'But do you think that once the Allemane have knocked out the French and the Jews, they'll push south and come down to Fez?' Zin's answer was vague; he said that the newspapers did not mention anything about the Allemane's long-term plans.

That night, Samir begged his mother to promise to put henna in his hair, in order to redden it, the next time we went to the *hammam* (public baths), and I ran around with one of my mother's scarves securely tied around my head, until she noticed it and forced me to take it off. 'Don't you ever cover your head!' Mother shouted. 'Do you understand me? Never! I am fighting against the veil, and you are putting one on?! What is this nonsense?' I explained to her about the Jews and the Allemane, the bombs and the submarines, but she was not impressed. 'Even if Hi-Hitler, the Almighty King of the Allemane, is after you,' she said, 'you ought to face him with your hair uncovered. Covering your head and hiding will not help. Hiding does not solve a woman's problems. It just identifies her as an easy victim. Your Grandmother and I have suffered enough of this head-covering business. We know it does not work. I want my daughters to stand up with their heads erect, and walk on Allah's planet with their eyes on the stars.' With that, she snatched off the scarf, and left me totally defenseless, facing an invisible army that was running after people with dark hair.

12

Asmahan, the Singing Princess

Sometimes, in the late afternoons, as soon as the men left the house, the women would jump to the radio, unlock it with their illegal key, and start a frantic search for music and love songs. Chama was the technician, since she could spell out the foreign letters inscribed in gold on the impressive radio face. Or so it seemed. The men manipulated the dials with smooth precise gestures, diciphering those mysterious signs, but although Chama had taught herself the French alphabet, she could not decode what *SW* (short wave), *MW* (medium wave), and *LW* (long wave) meant. She begged her brothers Zin and Jawad to tell her what the letters stood for, and when they refused, threatened to swallow the French dictionary whole. They told her that even if she did, she would still face the same problem, because those letters represented English words. She then gave up on the scientific approach, and developed an extraordinary fiddling technique, manipulating many dials at the same time, and pitilessly choking off all news stations, nationalist sermons, and military songs in search of a melody. Once the melody was caught, there was even more fiddling to be done – tuning that big radio to a distinct, static-free signal took forever.

But when Chama finally succeeded, and a warm and tender masculine voice, such as that of Abdelwahab the Egyptian crooning '*Ahibi 'itchi l-hurriya*' (I love the free, unshackled life) filled the air, the entire courtyard would start moaning and purring with delight. Even better was when Chama's magic fingers captured the ravishing voice of Princess Asmahan of Lebanon, whispering on the air waves, '*Ahwa! Ana, ana, ana, ahwa!*' (I am in love! I, I, I am in love!). Then, the women would be in pure ecstasy. They would toss their slippers away and dance barefooted in procession around the fountain, with one hand holding up their caftans, and the other hugging an imaginary male partner.

Unfortunately, however, Asmahan's melodies were hard to come by. Much more frequently, we heard the nationalistic anthems sung by Oum Kelthoum, an Egyptian diva who could warble for hours about the Arabs' grand past and the need for us to regain our glory by standing up to the colonial invaders.

Such a difference between Oum Kelthoum, a poor girl with a golden voice who was discovered in an obscure Egyptian village, and made her way to stardom through discipline and hard work, and the aristocratic Asmahan, who never had to exert any effort at all to attract fame! Oum Kelthoum projected the image of an unusually determined, self-assured Arab woman who had a purpose in life, and knew what she was doing, while Asmahan made our hearts sink with self-doubt and bewilderment. Solid and well-endowed (in the Boujeloud Cinema films, Oum Kelthoum always appeared in long, flowing robes which hid her motherly bosom), Oum Kelthoum thought about all the right and noble things – the Arabs' plight and their pain in a humiliating present – and gave voice to our nationalist yearnings for independence. Still, the women did not love her the way they loved Asmahan.

Asmahan was the exact opposite of Oum Kelthoum. A small-chested and lanky woman who often looked both completely confused and desperately elegant, she dressed in low-cut Western blouses and short skirts. Asmahan was oblivious of Arab culture, past and present, and totally absorbed by her own fatally tragic quest for happiness. She could not have cared less about what happened on the planet. All she wanted was to dress up, put flowers in her hair, look dreamy, sing, and dance away in the arms of a loving man, who would be as romantic as she – a warm and affectionate man who had the courage to split away from the group, and dance publicly with the woman he loved. Arab women, forced to dance alone in closed-off courtyards, admired Asmahan for realizing their dreams of hugging a man close in a Western-style dance, and swaying with him in a tight embrace. Aimless enjoyment, with a man by your side also totally engaged in the same, was the image that Asmahan projected.

Asmahan always had a pearl necklace around her long neck, and I would beg Chama to let me wear hers for a few minutes at a time, just to create some mysterious link between me and my idol. Once, I dared to ask Chama if there were any chance for me to marry an Arab prince like Asmahan, and she said the Arab world was heading towards democracy, and the rare princes available would be bad dancers, 'they would be totally absorbed by politics. Look for a teacher if you want to dance like Asmahan.'

We all knew about Asmahan's life in great detail, because Chama would constantly stage it in the plays she organized on the terrace. She would stage the lives of all kinds of heroines, but the romantic Princess was by far the most popular. Her life was as fascinating as any fairy tale, although it had a tragic end, as one could expect – an Arab woman could not seek sensuous enjoyment, frivolous entertainment, and happiness and get away with it. Asmahan was a princess born in Lebanon, in the Druze Mountains. Married at a very young age to her own cousin, a rich prince named Hassan, she was divorced at age seventeen, and dead at age thirty-two (in 1944), killed in a mysterious car accident involving international spies. In between, she was a singer and an actress living in Cairo, where she became an instant sensation throughout the Arab world. She entranced crowds with an unheard-of dream, that of individual happiness and of a sensuous, self-indulgent life, oblivious to the demands of the clan and its codes.

Asmahan practiced what she believed in, and what she sang. She thought that a woman could have both love and a career and insisted on living a full conjugal life while at the same time exploring and exhibiting her talents as an actress and a singer. Her first husband, Prince Hassan, could not accept that and divorced her. She tried again, twice, and in both cases, her husbands, both magnates of the Egyptian entertainment industry, began by giving in to her wishes. But soon, those marriages also ended up in outrageous divorces, with her last husband running after her with a gun and all the Cairo police following them and trying to stop him. Her final involvement with British and French intelligence agents, in their attempt to block the German presence in the Middle East, made her an easy target for moralistic attacks, and a defenseless victim of the region's explosive politics.

Then for a few years, back in Lebanon, Asmahan seemed finally to have found a place for herself. She looked beautiful, independent, and happy. She hosted high-powered meetings at her private residence in Beirut and at the King David Palace in Jerusalem between General de Gaulle of France and the President of Syria and Lebanon. At her eclectic soirées, Arab nationalists met European generals of the Allied Forces, and aspiring revolutionaries mingled with bankers.

Asmahan lived life on the run, tasted everything in a rush. 'I know my life is going to be short,' she always said. She earned plenty of money but never seemed to have enough to pay bills for her expensive jewels and dresses, and her capricious travels. She often impulsively decided to go on an unplanned journey, one of her favorite pastimes and one which constantly surprised her entourage. And it was during one of those spontaneous trips, when she was traveling by car with a female friend a few hundred miles out of Cairo, that death suddenly caught up with her. The car was found floating in a lake. Asmahan's fans mourned her while her enemies spoke of a conspiracy involving spies. Some said that she'd been killed by British intelligence because she had started acting too independently. Others dismissed her as a victim of German intelligence. Still others, self-appointed righteous bigots, congratulated themselves on her untimely death, calling it a just punishment for her disgraceful life.

Still, after her death, Asmahan became even more of a legend than ever because she showed Arab women that a life filled with deliberate self-indulgence, as short and scandalous as it might be, was better than a long and respectable one devoted to a lethargic tradition. Asmahan entranced both men and women with the idea that failure or success did not matter in the adventurous life and such a life was much more enjoyable than a life spent sleeping behind protective doors. You could not hum one of her songs without fragments of her incredibly exciting, albeit short and tragic life popping into your mind.

When Chama staged the first part of Asmahan's life, she threw a green carpet on the terrace floor so that we could visualize the forests of the steep Druze Mountains where Asmahan was born. Chama then pulled a sofa onto the stage to represent the Princess's bed, and smudged kohl powder around her eyes to suggest the Princess's dreamy green ones. The hair was more of a problem – the heroine's had been jet black – and so Chama was obliged to pull a charcoal-colored turban over her disturbingly red locks. There was not much she could do about her freckles, however, and Asmahan had had the clearest of skins. Instead, Chama concentrated on re-creating the actress's famed beauty spot on the left side of her chin. It would have been impossible to play her without it. Chama would then recline on the sofa, dressed in a satin *qamis* which was stretched out at the bottom with wire, so as to suggest a romantic Western dress. With a sad and gloomy look, she would stare at the sky in silence for a while. Then, voices behind the drapes would start singing a wistful melody about what an absurd waste of time it was to be lying there, when fun was going on everywhere else. The lovely voices belonged to Chama's sisters and other cousins.

A wooden horse would be standing near Asmahan's bed. For, you see, Asmahan had started running early in life. What else could a woman do who was born extremely beautiful into a princely family in a remote Arab region where everyone still remembered the crusades of long ago, dreaded foreign occupation, and watched a woman's every move? Asmahan rode horses like Tamou in the war-torn Rif zone; to her, liberation meant running. To be free was to be on the move. Riding fast, even when you had no purpose, could give you a taste of happiness – movement for the sheer joy of it. So Chama would get off the bed and ride the immobile horse, while the voices behind the drapes continued to sing about how depressing it felt to be trapped in a dead-end situation. Sometimes Samir or I would push the horse back and forth a few times to give the scene a sense of movement, while the audience (consisting of Mother, my adolescent cousins, Aunt Habiba, and all the other divorced and widowed aunts and relatives) sang along with the chorus.

Next, Samir and I would pull the drapes so that we could switch to the marriage scene. Chama did not like to see her audience sinking into despair for long. 'Escape from bad feelings ought to be the focus of entertainment,' she said. Cousin Zin would appear, dressed in a white cape, playing the part of the groom, Prince Hassan. At the sight of Zin's beauty, I would swoon and neglect my duties as a stage technician. And then the audience would start to complain, because it was the technicians' responsibility to provide refreshments whenever an important event, such as a marriage or birth, was taking place. Samir and I were in charge of the cookies. At one point, the audience also requested tea to go with the cookies, and threatened to strike if Chama did not provide it. But so many glasses got broken that Grandmother Lalla Mani intervened and prevented us from ever serving tea again. 'Theater is a sinful activity to begin with,' she said. 'It is not mentioned in the Koran, and no one ever heard about it in either Mecca or Medina. Now, if careless women still insist on indulging in theater, so be it. Allah will make everyone pay for their sins on Judgment Day. But breaking my son's tea glasses just because Asmahan, that scandalous lazybones is getting married, is utter recklessness.' After this, the theater marriages had to be celebrated in a very ascetic fashion and so we handed out small cookies, often prepared by Aunt Habiba, at the last minute. You had to treat the audience well, if you wanted them to stick around.

But to return to the play. You had not even finished your cookies when Prince Hassan threw out Asmahan, and Chama appeared on stage, with death-like powdered cheeks, carrying a big trunk, on her way to Cairo. The chorus would sing about separation, painful weaning and exile, while Aunt Habiba would whisper to Mother, 'Asmahan was only seventeen when she got divorced. What a shame! But then it was her only chance to get out of those stifling Druze Mountains. When you think about it, divorce is always a kind of an advancement. It forces you to take on adventure, which most of the time, you could do without.'

What made it all especially interesting, was that Prince Hassan threw his wife out because she wanted him to take her to cabarets and out dancing! Not only did she wear Western-style dresses with low necklines, high heels, and short hair, but she also wanted to frequent dance halls where people sat in stiff Western chairs around high tables, and talked nonsense or danced until dawn. During this scene, Chama would walk forward on the stage, pale and quivering, with her eyes half closed. 'Asmahan wanted to go to chic restaurants, dance like the French, and hold her Prince in her arms,' she would say. 'She wanted to waltz away with him all night, instead of standing on the sidelines behind curtains watching him deliberate in endless, exclusively male tribal counsels. She hated the whole clan and its senseless, cruel law. All she wanted was to drift away into bubble-like moments of happiness and sensual bliss. The lady was no criminal, she meant no harm.'

At this point, Aunt Habiba would interrupt the show. 'I never dreamed of such things,' she would chant, imitating one of Asmahan's melodies, 'And I got divorced just the same! So remember ladies, please, don't restrict yourselves. An Arab woman who does not go after the moon is a total idiot.'

'Be quiet!' everyone would call out, and then Chama would resume her dramatization of Asmahan's sensuous quest for romance in a society where the veil choked women's most elementary whims. As I watched Chama perform, I vowed to myself that when I became a grownup woman as tall as she, I definitely would be affiliated with a theater of some sort. I would dazzle Arab crowds, neatly seated in rows and looking up at me, and tell them about how it felt to be a woman intoxicated with dreams in a land that crushes both the dreams and the dreamer. I would make them cry over wasted opportunities, senseless captivities, smashed visions. And then, once they were on the same wavelength as I, I would, like Asmahan and Chama, sing of the wonders of self-exploration and the thrills of adventurous leaps into the unknown.

Oh, yes I would tell them about the impossible, about a new Arab world, in which men and women could hug each other and dance away, with no frontiers between them, and no fears.

Oh, yes, I would enchant my audience, and re-create, through magic words and calculated gestures, just like Asmahan and Chama before me, a serene planet on which houses had no gates, and windows opened wide onto safe streets.

I would help them walk in a world where the difference needed no veil, and where women's bodies moved naturally, and their desires created no anguish.

I would create for and with the audience, long poems about the absence of fear. Trust would be the new game we could explore, and I would humbly confess that I knew nothing of it either.

In my theater, I would earn enough money to serve tea and cookies to the audience, so that people could sit and relax for long hours while digesting the novel idea of a planet on which people walked without fears.

Just walking without feeling the chilling need for veils and boundaries.

Just walking, one foot in front of the other, with eyes riveted on a new, barely imaginable horizon of unthreatening strangeness.

I would convince everyone that happiness could flourish everywhere, even in the dark alleys of the aggressed Medinas.

Asmahan, I would re-claim her. She could exist, and not only as a tragic victim. Asmahans could thrive, and need not die at age thirty-two, in obscure foreign plots and senseless car accidents.

I shed many tears over Asmahan's tragic life during those afternoon theater sessions on that remote terrace. I assisted Chama in her short-lived Lebanese adventures, while at the same time keeping an eye on the shifting stars up above my head. Theater, that spelling out of dreams and giving up of body to fantasy, was so essential. I wondered why it was not declared a sacred institution.

13

The Harem Goes To The Movies

Although often dismissed as trivial, in our house, entertainment drew crowds. As soon as the women finished their domestic chores, they would rush to inquire where Aunt Habiba was telling her stories, or where Chama was presenting her plays. Entertainment thrived in out-of-the-way spaces, top floors, and terraces. Everyone was supposed to bring along a *glissa* (cushion) to sit on, and tried to find a good spot up front, on the carpet which defined the audience space. But many did not respect this rule, and brought stools instead. They were forced to sit in the back.

Seated comfortably on my cushion, with my legs crossed, I journeyed all over the world, hopping from one island to the next on boats that were always being wrecked and then miraculously set afloat again by resourceful princesses. When the excitement got really intense, I would take my cushion into my lap and rock back and forth, riding spellbound on the strange words being tossed out at the audience by Chama and Aunt

Habiba, the high priestesses of imagination. Aunt Habiba was certain that we all had magic inside, woven into our dreams. 'When you happen to be trapped powerless behind walls, stuck in a dead-end harem,' she would say, 'you dream of escape. And magic flourishes when you spell out that dream and make the frontiers vanish. Dreams can change your life, and eventually the world. Liberation starts with images dancing in your little head, and you can translate those images in words. And words cost nothing!' She constantly kept hammering at us about this magic within, saying that it was all our fault if we did not make the effort to bring it out. I could make frontiers vanish too – that was the message I got, sitting on my cushion, up on that terrace. It all seemed so natural was I rocked myself back and forth, throwing my head back occasionally to feel the starlight shining on my face. Theaters ought to be always situated high up, on white-washed terraces, near the skies. In Fez, on summer nights, faraway galaxies joined in our theater, and there were no limits to hope.

Oh, yes, Aunt Habiba, I thought, I will be a magician.
I will cross past this strictly codified life waiting for me in the narrow Medina streets, with my eyes fixed on the dream.
I will glide through adolescence, holding escape close to my chest, like the young European girls hold their dance partners close to theirs.
Words, I will cherish.
I will cultivate them to illuminate the nights,
Demolish walls
And dwarf gates.
It all seems easy, Aunt Habiba, with you and Chama going in and out of the fragile draped theater,
So frail in the late night, on that remote terrace.
But so vital, so nourishing, so wonderful.
I will become a magician.
I will chisel words to share the dream and render the frontiers useless.

During the day, Chama and Aunt Habiba waited patiently for the night, when they could summon imagination and arouse dreams, while sleep knocked out the less curious among us. Many of the women of the household lived for those nights, but the young men, sometimes called upon to take part in our plays, never responded with more than a mild enthusiasm. They did not care that much for storytelling and theater, for they, unlike the women, had unlimited access to our neighborhood Boujeloud Cinema, located next door to the *hammam*.

You knew that the young men were going to the movies when you saw Zin and Jawad put on their red bow ties. Often Chama would try to follow her brothers, begging them to take her along. Reluctant, they would argue that she had not gotten permission from either her own father or from mine. But she would try to follow them anyway, hurriedly putting on her *djellaba*, veiling her face with a black chiffon scarf, and rushing to the door behind them. Ahmed the doorkeeper would stand up as soon as he saw her. 'Chama,' he would say, 'Please don't force me to run after you in the street again today. I have no instructions to let women out.' But Chama would just keep on walking, as if she did not hear, and sometimes she did manage to slip out, so fast was she. Then all the courtyard women would flock to the hall to see what would happen next. A few minutes later, you saw Ahmed panting and puffing very loudly as he pushed Chama through the door. 'I have not been instructed that women were going to the movies,' he would repeat firmly. 'So, please, don't create trouble for me, don't force me to run at my age.'

Mother would get very agitated when Chama failed to escape and was brought back like a criminal. 'You wait and see, Ahmed,' she would prophesize, 'very soon you'll lose your job, for women will be free to run around the world.' She would then put her arm around Chama and cross the hall back to the courtyard, with all the other women following behind and mumbling about rebellion and punishment. Chama would remain silent, big tears running down her cheeks, and after a while, she would ask Mother in total bewilderment, 'I am seventeen and I can't see a movie because I am a woman! What justice is this? Who is going to lose in this Arab world if girls and boys are treated equally?'

Only when a film was a big hit, and the entire population of Fez turned out to see it, were the Mernissi women allowed to go too. That was the case with all of Asmahan's films, and with the film *Dananir*, about the singing *jarya*, or slave girl, who so captivated Caliph Harun al-Rashid with her voice and wit that he forgot all about his other one thousand *jarya*. Dananir was played by Oum Kelthoum, and brought to life by her incredibly powerful voice.

Dananir was based on history. Caliph Harun met a beautiful slave girl named Dananir during a *samar* evening. *Samar* was a sleepless night when an overworked caliph tried to relax and listen to poetry and music, either before or after important events, such as battles, dangerous voyages, and difficult negotiations. The most talented of artists were summoned to the palace, and since women were allowed to compete with men in these affairs, very soon Baghdad's *jarya* outpaced their male teachers, and *samar* became a women's affair. It was the opposite of a battlefield.

Caliph Harun badly needed to relax, because he spent most of his days fighting. During his reign, the Muslim empire stretched as far as China. But when it came to Dananir, Caliph Harun had a problem. She belonged to his own vizier, the highest official in his court, Yahya Ibn Khaled al-Barmaki.[1] And the Vizier loved

---

[1] The Barmaki family was very powerful at that time, and although

Dananir. So the Caliph kept his feelings for Dananir secret, and started visiting the Vizier regularly, in hopes of hearing Dananir's voice again. He could not openly acknowledge the love she inspired in him, but before long the entire city of Baghdad knew his secret anyway, and eleven hundred years later, the city of Fez still flocked to the movie theaters to witness his thwarted love, as filmed by Egyptian studios.

We children were not usually allowed to go to the movies either, but we staged our own revolts, just like the women, and sometimes were finally granted permission. When I say 'we,' I mean Samir really, for I had a problem with screaming at grownups and showing my displeasure by jumping up and down like he did, or better still, rolling on the floor and kicking bystanders. Staging sedition was a tricky business and never stopped being so for me, if only because of Mother's strange attitude. Often she encouraged me to rebel, and kept repeating that relying on Samir to be aggressive for the both of us would not do. But whenever I threw myself on the floor and started screaming at her, she would stop me on the spot. 'I did not say you ought to rebel against me! You should rebel against all the others, but you still have to obey your mother. Otherwise, it will lead to chaos. And in any case, you shouldn't rebel stupidly. You ought to carefully consider the situation, and analyze everything. Rebel when you know there is some chance you may win.' After that, I spent much energy analyzing my chances to win whenever it became evident that people were taking advantage of me, but even today, almost half a century later, the answers I come up with are always the same: inconclusive. I still dream of that wonderful day when I will stage a theatrical revolt 'Samir style', with screams and kicking feet. Looking back, I feel

Yahya was Harun's vizier, before that, he had been his teacher and mentor. Yahya died in the year 190 of the Hejira (A.D. ninth century).

so grateful that Samir did the right thing then. Otherwise I would never have gone to the movies.

And going to the movies was a thrill, from beginning to end. Women would dress up as if they were about to parade, unveiled, through the streets. Mother would spend hours and hours putting on her make-up and curling her hair in an incredibly complicated fashion. Elsewhere, in all the four corners of the courtyard, the other women would be feverishly making themselves up, too, with children holding mirrors and friends giving advice regarding kohl, rouge, hairstyles, and jewelry. The children had to hold the hand mirrors and angle them just right to catch the rays of the sun because the mirrors embedded in the salon's walls were not of much use at all. The sunlight hardly ever reached them, except for a few hours in the summer.

But finally, the women would be beautifully dressed. And then, they would cover themselves completely, from head to toe, with the veil and a *haik*, or *djellaba*, according to age and status!

Several years before, Mother had fought Father, first about the fabric that the veil was made of and then about the *haik*, or traditional long cloak that women wore in public.

The traditional veil was a rectangular piece of white cotton so heavy that it made the simple act of breathing a real accomplishment. Mother wanted to replace it with a tiny triangular black veil made of sheer silk chiffon. This drove Father crazy: 'It is so transparent! You might as well go unveiled!' But soon the small veil, the *litham*, became the fashion, with all the nationalists' wives wearing it all over Fez – to gatherings in the mosque and to public celebrations, such as when political prisoners were liberated by the French.

Mother also wanted to replace the traditional women's *haik* with the *djellaba*, or men's coat, which many of the nationalists' wives had taken to wearing as well. The *haik* was made of seven long meters of heavy white cotton cloth that you had to drape around yourself. You then had to hold on to the ends of the *haik*, awkwardly tied up under your chin, to keep it from falling off. 'The *haik*,' said Chama, 'was probably designed to make a woman's trip through the streets so torturous that she would quickly tire from the effort, rush back home, and never dream of going out again.' Mother hated the *haik*, too. 'If your foot slips, and you fall,' she said, 'you are likely to lose your teeth, because you have your hands tied up. Besides, it is so heavy, and I am so skinny!' The *djellaba*, on the other hand, was a closely fitted man's robe with a hood, slits in the sides to allow long strides, and trimmed sleeves which left your hands completely free. When the nationalists first started sending their daughters to school, they also started letting them wear the *djellaba* because it was so much lighter and more practical than the *haik*. Going back and forth to school four times a day was not like going to visit a saint's tomb once a year. So the daughters started wearing the men's *djellaba*, and soon thereafter, their mothers followed suit. To discourage Mother from joining in, Father commented regularly on the revolution that he was witnessing in the Medina streets. 'It is like the French women trading their skirts for men's pants,' he said. 'And if women dress like men, it is more than chaos, it is *fana* (the end of the world).'

But slowly and gradually, the chaos in the streets spread to our house, and the planet miraculously continued to turn as usual. One day, Mother appeared wearing Father's *djellaba*, the hood neatly folded up on her forehead, and a tiny triangular black *litham* made of sheer silk chiffon hanging loosely over her nose. Of course, anyone could see right through that veil, and Father angrily warned her that she was destroying the family honor. But family honor suddenly seemed to be in serious jeopardy all over Fez, because the Medina streets were flooded by women wearing the men's *djellaba* with coquettish chiffon veils. Not long after that, too, the daughters of the nationalists began appearing in the streets with bare faces and bare legs, in Western dresses with the distinctive Western handbags on their shoulders. Of course, Mother could not dream of taking up Western dress, so conservative was her immediate environment, but she was able to keep her *djellaba* and the sheer chiffon *litham*. Later, in 1956, as soon as Mother heard that Morocco had gotten independence and the French armies were leaving, she joined the march organized by the nationalists' wives, and sang with them until late in the night. When she finally came home exhausted from walking and singing, her hair was uncovered and her face was bare. From then on, there were no more black *litham* to be seen covering young women's faces in Fez Medina; only old ladies and young, newly migrant peasants kept the veil.[2]

But to get back to the movies. On those rare festive days, the women's procession would leave the house in the early afternoon, with my male cousins in front, as if to prevent a crowd from gathering around and trying to catch a rare glimpse of the Mernissi beauties. Just after the men would come Grandmother Lalla Mani with her *haik* majestically draped around her tiny silhouette, and her head held disdainfully high, as if to let even anonymous passersby know that she was a woman of authority. Lalla Radia, Samir's mother, would be walking by Grandmother's side and taking meticulously measured steps, her eyes on the pavement. Behind them would come Aunt Habiba and all

[2] While upper- and middle-class women threw away the veil, the newly migrant peasant women who came to Fez after independence would wear one to proclaim their 'urbanity,' to show that they belonged to the city and were no longer part of the countryside where the veil was never, throughout North Africa, worn by women. Even today, the highly political Islamic *hijab*, which is a distinct headdress, is an urban, middle class, educated phenomenon in Morocco. Peasant and working class women do not join in that fashion.

the widowed and divorced relatives, each walking in total silence and holding tightly onto her white *haik*. Unlike Mother, the widowed and divorced women, with no husbands to protect them, could not claim the right to wear *djellabas*. To have done so would have meant immediate and irreversible condemnation as loose women. In the last rows of the procession would come the rebels, each dressed in a tight, colorful *djellaba*, followed by the shy adolescent cousins who would giggle nervously all the way to the cinema, and finally we children, holding Ahmed's hands.

There were not really many women in the rebels section, only Mother and Chama, but they managed to get everyone's attention. Mother, with her kohl-lined eyes, and Chama, with her false Asmahan beauty spot, were veiled, yes, in that they wore the tiny, transparent black *litham*, but their hands were free, and sensuous perfumes were floating provocatively in the air around them. Often, Mother would make everyone burst out laughing by imitating Leila Mourad, the Egyptian movie star whose specialty was to play the femme fatale. She would walk while staring straight ahead (at the risk of tripping over the sharp stones which paved the Medina streets), open her eyes very wide, as if she had a dangerous eye infection, and then dart her gaze to the left and right, sending deadly magnetic rays, as she whispered in a conspiratorial tone, 'No men can resist my awesome beauty! A single second of eye contact, and innocent victims will fall wriggling on the ground. There is going to be manslaughter in the streets of Fez today!'

Mother had come up with that idea after hearing the theories of an Egyptian male feminist writer named Qacem Amin. He was the author of a bestseller, provocatively entitled *The Liberation of the Women* (1899, year 1316 of the Muslim calendar), in which he hypothesized that men veiled women because they were afraid of their charm and beauty. Men could not resist women, he wrote, and often felt faint whenever a beautiful one came gliding by. Qacem Amin concluded his book by urging Arab men to find ways to develop strength within themselves and overcome their fears, so that women could shed the veil. Mother loved Qacem Amin, but since she was illiterate, she had to beg Father to read her favorite passages to her. Before giving in, Father would make all kinds of requests, which she at first would refuse to grant, such as holding his hand while he was reading, making his favorite drink (a milk shake with freshly crushed almonds and a drop of orange flower essence), or even worse, giving him a foot massage. Eventually, though, Mother reluctantly would grant his wish, and urge him to begin reading. Then, just when she was starting to enjoy herself, Father suddenly would stop, toss the book away, and complain that Qacem Amin was destroying the harmony of Arab marriage. 'I need the help of this Egyptian nut to get closer to my wife, and to have her be nice to me?' he would complain. 'I can't believe it!' Then Mother would rush to pick the book up off the floor, put it back into its leather cover, and leave the room, sulky but sure of herself, with her treasure under her arm.

Chama, with her freckles and honey-colored eyes, would laugh delightedly whenever Mother put on her femme fatale act as they walked from the house to the cinema. They would both look carefully to the left and the right to see if any passersby were about to fall down on the ground. And of course, both women would also comment on the men they passed, causing Cousin Zin and his brothers to turn around from time to time and ask them not to talk so loud.

Once in the cinema, the whole harem would sit in two rows, having tickets for four, in order to leave the row in front, as well as the one behind, unoccupied. We did not want some mischievous, irreverent cinema-goer to take advantage of the darkness and pinch one of the ladies while she was engrossed in the movie plot.

14

Egyptian Feminists Visit
the Terrace

Many of the plays staged by Chama on the terrace required male actors, and when there was no competition from the neighborhood cinema, all the young men of the house would join in. Zin, of course, was very much in demand, because of his grace and eloquence. And he took great pleasure in stealing Uncle's and Father's turbans and capes, and in fashioning a variety of wooden swords so he could play the Abbasid princes convincingly. He also played numerous other roles, from pre-Islamic poets to modern nationalist heroes held captive in French and British jails. The plays which thrilled the audience the most, however, were those which involved great crowd scenes, and much marching and singing, because then everyone could participate. These scenes drove Chama crazy, because they meant that at times, the audience would completely vanish. 'You have to have someone sitting there to see the play!' she would argue. 'You can't have a theater without an audience!' The problem with Chama was that she was subject to wildly unpredictible mood swings, and could go from bubbling excitement one moment to deep silence the next, without any outward sign that the change was imminent. She also got discouraged very easily when the audience did not behave, and then she would simply stop in the middle of a sentence, look sadly at those who had created the interruptions, and walk towards the stairs. There was not much you could do about it either, and sometimes she would remain depressed for days, keeping to her room. But when Chama was in a good mood, she could inflame the entire house for sure!

For you see, Chama's theater provided wonderful opportunities for all of us to discover and show our talents, overcome our shyness and develop some self-confidence. My normally very shy adolescent girl cousins, for example, got their chance to shine when they sang in the chorus. They hated it when the drapes were up – then they would salute the audience, while fiddling nervously with their braids – but when the drapes were down, their voices would ring out, clear and lovely. I, on the other hand, became absolutely indispensable when Chama discovered that I could do acrobatic leaps (I had learned them from Grandmother Yasmina). From then on, my acrobatics entertained the audience whenever things got out of hand. As soon as I sensed something going wrong between the director, or the actors, and the audience, I would get up on stage with my legs in the air and my hands on the ground. I learned to recognize instinctively when Chama was about to fall into a sad mood. My acrobatics also allowed the actors to make lengthy costume changes between scenes. Without my assistance, Chama would have had to cut back on her elaborate preparations.

I was very proud to have a role to play, even though it was a silent and marginal one, and one which involved mostly my feet. But Aunt Habiba said it did not matter what role you played, as long as you were useful. The essential thing was to have a role, to contribute to a common goal. Besides, she said,

I would soon have a bigger role to play in real life; all I needed was to develop a talent. I told her that acrobatics would probably be that talent, but she was not convinced. 'Real life is tougher than theater,' she said. 'Besides, our tradition requires women to walk on their feet. Throwing them up in the air is a rather delicate matter.' That was when I started to worry about my future.

But Aunt Habiba said not to worry, that everyone had wonderful things hidden inside. The only difference was that some managed to share those wonderful things, and others did not. Those who did not explore and share the precious gifts within went through life feeling miserable, sad, awkward with others, and angry too. You had to develop a talent, Aunt Habiba said, so that you could give something, share, and shine. And you developed a talent by working very hard at becoming good at something. It could be anything – singing, dancing, cooking, embroidering, listening, looking, smiling, waiting, accepting, dreaming, rebelling, leaping. 'Anything you can do well can change your life,' said Aunt Habiba.

So I decided that I would develop a talent and give happiness to those around me. Then no one could hurt me, could they? The only problem was that I did not know yet what my talent was. But I was sure I had something inside. Allah is generous and gives every one of his creatures some beautiful thing, tucking it right inside, like a mysterious flower, without you even knowing it. I had probably received my share, and would just have to wait and develop it when the right time came. Meanwhile, I would learn all I could from the heroines of literature and history.

The heroines most often portrayed in Chama's theater were, in order of frequency: Asmahan, the actress and singer, the Egyptian and Lebanese feminists; Scheherazade and the princesses of *A Thousand and One Nights*; and finally, important religious figures.

Among the feminists, or *ra-idates* – pioneers of women's rights –
three were special favorites of Chama: Aisha Taymour, Zaynab
Fawwaz, and Huda Sha°raoui.[1] Among the religious figures, the
most popular were Khadija and Aisha, the wives of the Prophet
Mohammed and Rabea al-Adaouiya, a mystic. Their lives were
usually staged during Ramadan, when Grandmother Lalla Mani
would dress entirely in green, the color of the Prophet, Allah's
Prayer and Peace be Upon Him, and go into a deep mystical
meditation. Then, she would preach repentance from sin, and
predict hell for everyone forgetful of Allah's commands in
general, and for women who wanted to discard the veil, dance,
sing, and have fun in particular.

Moroccan women, thirsty for liberation and change, had to
export their feminists from the East, for there were no local ones
as yet famous enough to become public figures and nurture their
dreams. 'No wonder Morocco is so far behind,' Chama would
remark from time to time. 'Squeezed between the silence of the
Sahara Desert in the South, the furious waves of the Atlantic
Ocean in the West, and the Christian invaders' aggression from

---

[1] Early feminists are quite famous in the Arab world, where there is a
strong tradition of documenting women's lives, accomplishments, and
exploits in the form of 'who's who' compilations. Arab historians' fascination with exceptional women has produced a distinct literary genre called
nissaiyyat, from the word *nissa*, or women. Salah al-Din al-Mounajid, an
admirer of outstanding women, listed some one hundred treatises on
women in his 'Ma ullifa 'ani an-nissa' (What Was Written on Women), in
the journal *Majallat majma al-lugha l-°Arabiyya* (1941), vol. 16, p. 216.
Unfortunately, the Arab feminists, who are key figures in the modern
history of human rights in the Muslim world, are hardly known in the
West. One very good profile of major Muslim feminists of the nineteenth
and early twentieth centuries, which could be very useful for Western
readers if translated, is the first volume of Emily Nasrallah's *Women
Pioneers*, which exists at the moment in Arabic only (Beirut: Muassassat
Nawfal, 1986).

the North, Moroccans recoiled in defensive attitudes, while all the other Muslim nations have sailed away into modernity. Women have advanced everywhere except here. We are a museum. We should make tourists pay a fee at the gates of Tangier!'

The problem with some of Chama's favorite feminists, especially the early ones, was that they did not do much besides write, since they were locked up in harems. That meant that there was not much action to be staged, and we just had to sit and listen to Chama recite their protests and complaints in monologue. The life of Aisha Taymour was the worst. Born in Cairo in 1840, all she did, nonstop until her death in 1906, was write fiery poetry against the veil. She wrote in many languages however – Arabic, Turkish, and even Persian – and that impressed me. A woman held hostage in a harem, speaking foreign languages! Speaking a foreign language is like opening a window in a blind wall. Speaking a foreign language in a harem is like developing wings that allow you to fly to another culture, even if the frontier is still there, and the gatekeeper too. When Chama wanted us to know that Aisha Taymour was reading her poetry in Turkish or Persian, languages no one in Fez Medina had ever heard or could understand, she would throw her head way back, fix her eyes on the ceiling or the sky, and start uttering unintelligible guttural nonsense, using the rhythms of Arabic poetry. That made Mother impatient. 'We have been enlightened, dear, and impressed with Aisha's mastery of Turkish,' she would say. 'Now switch to Arabic, or you'll lose your audience.' At that Chama would abruptly stop speaking, look very offended, and ask Mother to apologize at once. 'I am weaving delicate magic,' she would say, 'and if you keep shouting, you'll destroy the dream.' Mother would then stand up, bow her head and entire upper torso, raise it again, and swear that she would never again utter a misplaced word. For the rest of the drama, she would sit motionless, with a visibly appreciative smile on her face.

The other pioneering feminist whom Chama admired a lot, and we had to live with, was Zaynab Fawwaz, an erudite, self-taught Lebanese woman born in the 1850s, who rose from the status of an obscure village domestic to that of a famous literary figure in Beirut and Cairo intellectual circles, through a combination of strategically planned marriages and disciplined self-improvement. But since Zaynab never stepped out of her harem, transforming her truncated life into drama was awfully difficult. From her harem, all Zaynab Fawwaz could really do was inundate the Arab press with articles and poetry, in which she vented her hatred of the veil and condemned the seclusion of women. Both, she argued, were major obstacles to Muslim greatness, and both explained our mediocre performance when facing Western colonial armies. Fortunately, we on the terrace did not have to endure Zaynab's press releases, which were exceedingly repetitive, for long. She had also published a 'who's who' of famous women in 1893, in which she had collected more than four hundred and fifty dazzling, eclectic biographies of role models for women, from Cleopatra to Queen Victoria of England, and these gave Chama a lot of material to choose from.[2]

But the most successful pioneering champion of women's rights, as far as the terrace audience was concerned, was Huda Sha'raoui, an aristocratic Egyptian beauty, born in 1879, who bewitched Egypt's rulers with ardent speeches and popular street

---

[2] Zaynab Fawwaz al-Amili, *Al-Durr al-Manthour fi Tabaqat Rabbat al-Khodour* (Boulaq, Egypt: Al-Matba'a al-Kubra, 1895, year 1312 of the Muslim calendar). She explains in her introduction that her book is 'a work dedicated to the cause of female beings of my kind' (*ja'altuhu khidmatun li-banati naw'i*).

marches. Her life provided ample opportunity for everyone on the terrace, including us children, to get up on stage and chant nationalist military hymns. You needed actors to play the Egyptian protesters, actors to play the British police, and of course actors to play the bystanders.

Forced into an early marriage at age 13, Huda fascinated Chama because she was able to transform a whole society in just a few decades by sheer stubborn will. Huda managed to do two seemingly contradictory things at the same time – fight the British occupation and end her own traditional seclusion and confinement. She tossed away her veil when she led the first official women's street march against the British in 1919, and influenced legislators to pass numerous important laws, including one in 1924 which raised the legal marriage age for girls to 16. She also was so utterly disgusted by the newly independent Egyptian state, formed in 1922, when they passed the Constitution of 1923 restricting the vote to males, that she created the Egyptian Feminist Union and successfully fought for a woman's right to vote.[3] Huda Sha'raoui's stubborn insistence on women's rights inspired many other newly independent Arab nations, already attracted to the nationalists ideals, to include a woman's right to vote in their new constitutions as well.

On the terrace, we loved the 1919 women's street march. A key moment in the buildup of Chama's plot, it allowed almost everyone to invade the stage, push past the very shaky drapes

---

[3] Huda Sha'raoui is well-known in the Arab world, and a glimpse of her extraordinary life can be caught in Margot Badran's translation of a selection of her memoirs entitled *Harem Years: The Memoirs of an Egyptian Feminist* (London: Virago Press, 1986). For an illustrated description of Huda Sha'raoui's feminist campaigns, see Sarah Graham Brown, *Image of Women: The Portrayal of Women in Photography of the Middle East, 1860–1950* (New York: Columbia University Press, 1988). The last chapter, 'Campaigning Women,' contains photos of the 1919 women's march.

that Chama had had such difficulty putting up (they were supported by wash poles stuck in olive jars), jump up and down, shout insults at imaginary British soldiers, and toss away their scarves, symbols of the despised veils. We children, of course, had an especially wonderful time, entranced by the sight of all these grownups, including our own mothers, playing like kids. Often, things got so exhuberant that Chama would be forced to climb up onto the ladder used to set up the scenery, and shout that the actors would have to leave the stage, because the British had left Egypt in 1922 and it was now 1947. Huda was about to die and solemn silence was a must, because she had died peacefully in her bedroom. When, as was often the case, we did not budge from the stage, Chama's shouts turned to threats. 'If the actors do not come to their senses and respect the play's timing,' she would proclaim from the top of the ladder, 'the theater management is going to declare its doors shut for the entire summer, because of hooliganism, perpetrated by uncontrolled elements.'

Switching from the festive 1919 street march to Huda's deathbed scene was quite tricky. Not only did we have to leave the stage to become the audience once again, but we also had to show, through heavy silence, that we were in mourning. Not all of us could do it. Aunt Habiba was officially thrown off the terrace once because she could not resist laughing when Chama, rushing out from behind the drapes, covered in a hastily-put-on black sheet, tripped and lost her balance. Everyone else wanted to laugh, too, but luckily, Chama was so involved in regaining her equilibrium that she did not see our faces. Only Aunt Habiba made the mistake of laughing loud, and then Chama demanded that the audience help throw her out. We went along with Chama's request, because otherwise she would have declared a theater strike, and that would not have been in anyone's interest.

Deep down, though, the problem with feminists' lives was

that they did not have enough singing and dancing in them. Chama might have liked staging them, but the audience much preferred watching Asmahan or one of the adventurous heroines from *A Thousand and One Nights*. For one thing, those stories had more love, lust, and adventure in them. The feminists' lives seemed to be all about fighting and unhappy marriages, never about happy moments, beautiful nights, or whatever it was that gave them the strength to carry on. 'All these hyperactive ladies who pioneered new ideas fascinated Arab men,' said Aunt Habiba. 'Men were constantly falling in love with them, but we never hear a word about those enchanting embraces, either because feminists thought they were politically irrelevant, or because they censored themselves for fear of being attacked as immoral.' Sometimes, too, Aunt Habiba privately wondered if it were not Chama who did the censoring, afraid to dramatize the romantic parts for fear that the audience might drift off and forget about the struggle. Whatever the reason was, I decided then and there that if I ever led a battle for women's liberation, I definitely would not forget about sensuality. As Aunt Habiba said, 'Why rebel and change the world if you can't get what's missing in your life? And what is most definitely missing in our lives is love and lust. Why organize a revolution if the new world is going to be an emotional desert?'

Scheherazade's women of *A Thousand and One Nights* did not write about liberation – they went ahead and lived it, dangerously and sensuously, and they always succeeded in getting themselves out of trouble. They did not try to convince society to free them – they went ahead and freed themselves. Take the story of Princess Budur, for example. Here she was, a very spoiled and extremely over-protected princess, the daughter of mighty King Ghayur, and the wife of the equally powerful Prince Qamar al-Zaman. She set off on a journey with her husband, and of course he took care of everything; she was just following behind, as women do when traveling with their husbands and male relatives. They traveled a long way into foreign lands, and then, one day, Princess Budur woke up to find that she was all alone in her tent, in the middle of nowhere. The Prince Qamar had vanished. Afraid that the other men in the caravan might try to rape her, steal her jewelry, or even sell her into slavery, Princess Budur decided to dress in her husband's clothes and convince the others that she was a man. She was no longer Princess Budur, but Prince Qamar al-Zaman. And her ruse worked! Not only did she escape rape and dishonor, but she also was given a kingdom to rule.

The terrace cheered Princess Budur, because she dared to imagine the impossible, the unrealistic. As a woman, she was powerless and desperately weak, surrounded by tough highway robbers. In fact, her situation was really hopeless – she was stuck in the middle of nowhere, far away from home, in the midst of a whole caravan of untrustworthy slaves and eunuchs, not to mention dubious merchants. But when your situation is hopeless, all you can do is turn the world upside down, transform it according to your wishes, and create it anew. And that is precisely what Princess Budur did.

15

Princess Budur's Fate

If you looked for Princess Budur in *A Thousand and One Nights*, you would have a hard time finding her. First of all, her name does not appear in the table of contents. The story goes by her husband's name, 'The Tale of Qamar al-Zaman.' Second, her story is told on the nine hundred and sixty-second night, so you would have to read almost to the end of the book to find it. Aunt Habiba said that that could have been because Scheherazade, the author of the tales, was afraid of having her head chopped off if she had told the story of Princess Budur earlier.[1] The bottom line of her story, after all, was that a woman can fool society by posing as a man. All she has to do is to wear her husband's clothes; the difference between the sexes is silly, only a matter of

[1] In the Arabic text I have (Beirut: Al-Maktaba al-Cha'biya, vol. 4), 'The Tale of Qamar al-Zaman' starts on the nine hundred and sixty-second night, but in the Burton translation, it is on the one hundred and seventieth night.

dress. That indeed, was quite an insolent lesson for Scheherazade to narrate to angry King Schahriar, especially at the beginning. She had to soften him up first, by entertaining him with less threatening tales.

One very likeable quality of Princess Budur was that she was not strong. Like the majority of the women on the terrace, she was not a person who was accustomed to solving her own problems. Totally dependent on men, and completely ignorant of the world outside, she had never developed any self-assurance nor had any practice in analyzing problematic situations and coming up with solutions. Yet, in spite of her apparent helplessness, she made the right – and very daring – decisions. 'There is nothing wrong with being helpless, ladies!' Aunt Habiba would say, when it was her turn to take over the stage. 'Princess Budur's life is the proof. Not having had the opportunity to test your talents does not mean that you have none.'

Aunt Habiba took over the stage whenever the audience got bored with Chama's feminists and demanded more cheerful dramas that included singing and dancing. As a stage director, Aunt Habiba was not as compulsive as Chama, who invested an incredible amount of energy into the stage set and the costumes. Aunt Habiba, by contrast, reduced everything to the minimal. 'Life is already complicated enough as it is,' she would say. 'So, for God's sake, don't make things difficult when you want to relax.' During the dramas, Aunt Habiba would sit on a comfortable chair covered with a lavishly embroidered drape, to make it look like a throne. She also wore, for the occasion, her elegant gold embroidered caftan, which she usually kept carefully folded in the cedar chest that she had salvaged from her divorce. Made of black velvet and studded with pearls that her father had brought back from his pilgrimage to Mecca, the caftan had taken Aunt Habiba three years to embroider. 'Today, people buy ready-made clothes and go around wearing things they did not create,' she would say. 'But when you put many nights into embroidering a scarf or a caftan, it becomes a wonderful work of art.'[2] Surely, Aunt Habiba's caftan was unusually impressive, and since she only put it on for special occasions, you always felt as if you were somewhere else the moment she appeared wearing it on stage.

Princess Budur's drama started out well enough, with her father, King Ghayur, providing her and her loving husband, Prince Qamar al-Zaman, with everything they needed for their trip. The King

brought out of his stable horses marked with his own brand, blood dromedaries which can journey ten days without water, and prepared a litter for his daughter, besides loading mules and camels with victual; moreover, he gave them slaves and eunuchs to serve them and all manner of traveling gear, and on the day of departure, when King Ghayur took leave of Qamar al-Zaman, he bestowed on him ten splendid suits of cloth of gold embroidered with stones of price, together with ten riding horses and ten she-camels, and a treasury of money, and he charged him to love and cherish

---

[2] Although harems disappeared in the 1950s, and upper- and middle-class women moved into education and salaried positions, the desire of women to keep control over fashion remains, as strong as ever. The thousands of Moroccan women who are in the professions in the 1990s (one-third of the doctors, lawyers, and university professors in Morocco are women) did not give up the tradition of designing their clothes and jewelry, and have thus contributed to a revival of the traditional crafts. *Djellabas* and caftans have been shortened and redesigned according to taste and fantasies in all kinds of fabrics and colors. It is not uncommon to meet women doctors, judges, and lawyers in dark Medina alleys, sitting on craftsmen's stools and discussing the color, design, and embroidery of their modern clothes.

his daughter the lady Budur. [Then, the Prince and Princess
set out] without stopping through the first day and the
second and the third and the fourth; nor did they cease faring
for a whole month till they came to a spacious Champaign,
abounding in pasturage, where they pitched their tents; and
they ate and drank and rested, and the Princess Budur lay
down to sleep.[3]

And when she woke up the next morning, she was all by
herself in the tent. Her husband had mysteriously disappeared.

At this point, we children, sitting behind Princess Budur's
tent, would make all sorts of noises to indicate that the caravan
was waking up. Samir was superb at imitating the horse noises
and jumping about, and would only stop reluctantly when
Chama, as Princess Budur, started reflecting out loud about the
solitude and the powerlessness of a woman who suddenly finds
herself without a husband.

> If I go out and tell the valets and let them learn that my
> husband is lost, they will lust after me: there is no help for it
> but that I use stratagem. So she rose and donned some of her
> husband's clothes and riding-boots, and a turban like his,
> drawing one corner of it across her face for a mouth veil.
> Then, setting a slave-girl in her litter, she went forth from the
> tent [and along with her entourage, journeyed for days and
> nights] till they came in sight of a city overlooking the Salt
> Sea, where they pitched their tents without the walls and
> halted to rest. The Princess asked the name of the town and
> was told, 'It is called the City of Ebony, its King is named

[3] 'The Tale of Qamar al-Zaman,' Burton's translation, vol. 3, p. 278.

Armanus, and he hath a daughter Hayat al-Nufus.'[4]

Arriving at the City of Ebony did not bring an end to Princess Budur's troubles. In fact, her situation got worse because King Armanus was so pleased with the counterfeit Qamar al-Zaman that he wanted to marry her off to his own daughter, Hayat al-Nufus. What a horrifying prospect for Princess Budur! Hayat al-Nufus would discover her ruse immediately, and she might even be beheaded. People got beheaded in the City of Ebony for less than that every day.

In the next scene, Princess Budur paced back and forth in her tent, wondering what to do. If she accepted the King's proposition, she might be sentenced to death for lying. But if she refused the King's proposition, she might also be sentenced to death. You could not refuse a king's offer if you wanted to live a long and healthy life, especially when to refuse a King's offer meant snubbing his daughter.

While Chama paced back and forth, dramatizing Princess Budur's dilemma, the audience split into two camps. The first camp suggested that she tell the King the truth, because if she let him know that she was a woman, he might fall in love with her and pardon her. The second camp suggested that it would be safer for her to accept the offer of marriage and then tell Princess Hayat everything, once in the bridal suite, because that would trigger women's solidarity. Women's solidarity was actually a highly sensitive issue in the courtyard, since the women rarely sided all together against men. Some of the women, like Grandmother Lalla Mani and Lalla Radia, who were in favor of harems, always went along with the men's decisions, while women like Mother did not. In fact, Mother accused women

[4] Ibid., p. 283.

who allied themselves with men as being largely responsible for women's suffering. 'These women are more dangerous than men,' she would explain, 'because physically, they look just like us. But they are really wolves posing as sheep. If women's solidarity existed, we would not be stuck on this terrace. We would be traveling around Morocco or even sailing to the City of Ebony if we wanted to.' Aunt Habiba, who always sat in the front row, even when she did not herself direct or have a role to play, was charged by Chama to keep a tight surveillance over the audience's moods, and whenever the issue of women's solidarity came up, she censored it before it escalated into a serious, bitter argument.

At any rate, Princess Budur did choose women's solidarity, and it proved to be a very good choice, and one that demonstrated that women were capable of grand and noble sentiments towards one another. Princess Budur accepted King Armanus' proposal to marry his daughter, and this was an act which immediately gave her the right to become the ruler of the City of Ebony – not a bad start at all. We on the terrace celebrated the wedding, with Samir and I handing out cookies. Once, Chama tried to argue that since a marriage between two women is not legal, cookies need not be distributed. But the audience reacted at once. 'The cookie rule must be respected. You never mentioned that the marriage had to be legal.'

After the wedding, the newlyweds retired to Princess Hayat's bedroom. But that first night, Princess Budur kissed her bride a very quick good night and then started praying for hours on end until poor Hayat fell asleep. During this scene, we would be all laughing at Chama's portrayal of the very religious groom. 'Stop praying, and get on with the job,' Mother would shout. Then Samir and I would rush forward to let down the drapes and thereby show that one night had passed. Then we would raise the drapes again and the poor husband would still be praying while Hayat al-Nufus sat waiting to be kissed. We would do this again and again, with the husband always praying, the wife always waiting, and the whole audience roaring with laughter.

Finally, after many nights of prayer, Princess Hayat got fed up and went to complain to her powerful father, King Armanus. Prince Qamar, she said, was not interested in giving her a child, for he spent all his nights praying nonstop. As one might expect, this did not please the King and he threatened to banish the bridegroom from the City of Ebony immediately, if he did not start behaving as a man should. So that very night, Princess Budur confessed to Princess Hayat, telling her the whole story from beginning to end, and asked for her help. 'I conjure thee by Allah to keep my counsel, for I have concealed my case only that Allah may reunite me with my beloved Qamar al-Zaman.'[5]

And of course the miracle happened. Princess Hayat sympathized with Princess Budur and promised to help her. The two women then staged a false virginity ceremony, as tradition dictated.

> Hayat al-Nufus arose and took a pigeon-poult, and cut its throat over her smock and besmeared herself with its blood. Then she pulled off her petticoat-trousers and cried aloud, whereupon her people hastened to her and raised the usual lullilooing and outcries of joy and gladness.[6]

After that, the two women posed as husband and wife, with Princess Budur ruling the Kingdom with one hand, and organizing search parties to find her beloved Qamar al-Zaman with the other.

[5] Burton translation, p.289.

[6] Ibid.

The women on the terrace cheered at Princess Hayat's decision to help the distressed Budur, who had dared to do the impossible, and after the play was over, talked heatedly, long into the night, about fate and happiness, and how to escape the first and pursue the second. Women's solidarity, many agreed, was the key to both.

16

The Forbidden Terrace

Happiness, however, I thought then and still do now, is inconceivable without a terrace, and by a terrace I mean something very different from the European rooftops that Cousin Zin described after visiting Blad Teldj, or Snowland. He said that the houses up there did not have the neatly whitewashed, and sometimes sumptuously paved, flat terraces like our own, with sofas and plants and flowering shrubs. In contrast, their roofs were triangular and pointed because they had to shelter the houses from the snow, and you couldn't possibly stretch out on them because you would slide right off. Still, not all the terraces of Fez were meant to be accessible; the highest ones normally were declared off-limits, because you could die if you fell off them. Nonetheless, I dreamed constantly of visiting our forbidden terrace, which was the highest one on our street, and one where no child had ever been seen, as far as I could remember.

But the first time I finally climbed up onto that forbidden terrace, I forgot all about my dreams of visiting the place.

Instead, I decided right on the spot to reconsider the idea that grownups were always unreasonable and dead set against letting children be happy. I was even so scared, standing up there, that I lost the capacity to breathe and started trembling. I wished that I had obeyed the grownups after all, and had never left the banal lower terrace, surrounded by its two-meter-high walls. The minarets and even the huge Qaraouiyine Mosque crouched below me like tiny toys in a dwarf's city. Meanwhile, the clouds passing by overhead seemed menacingly close, with bright pink, almost red flames on their tops, which I had never seen from below. I heard a bizarre noise so frightening that, at first, I thought it was a monstrous, invisible bird. But when I asked Cousin Malika about it, she said that I was just scared; the noise was my own blood rushing through my veins, and she had felt the same way, the first time she had found herself on the forbidden terrace. But she also said that if I cried or said I was afraid, she would go so far as to help me down, but would never bring me up here with her again, and I would spend the rest of my life confused about the word 'harem.' That, you see, was the subject that she and Samir were planning to discuss on the terrace. They had given themselves the mission to analyze that elusive word, and as a reward, had treated themselves to a visit to the fabulous forbidden terrace. Total discretion was essential; they did not want anyone to know about the visit.

So I whispered that I was not afraid. All I needed was some advice about how to stop the noise in my head. She said that I should lie down, with my face up to the sky, avoid looking at moving objects, such as clouds or birds, and fix my eyes on a stable point. Then, if I concentrated on that point for a while, the world would return to normal. Before I lay down, I instructed her to let Mother know that, in case it was Allah's will that I die on the terrace, I owed huge sums of money to Sidi Sussi, the king of roasted chick-peas and charcoal-grilled peanuts and almonds, who had a stall outside our Koranic school. You would be sent directly to hell, my teacher Lalla Tam had told me, if you arrived in the other world with debts. A good Muslim always paid her debts and kept clean accounts, alive or dead.

The terrace above the one on which we staged our plays was forbidden because it had no walls, and you could fall and die with one false move. Five meters higher than the terrace below it, it was in fact, the very ceiling of Aunt Habiba's room. There were no stairs leading to it because it was not meant to be visited; the only official means of access was a ladder, kept by Ahmed the doorkeeper. But everyone in the house knew that troubled women who had *hem*, a kind of mild depression, climbed up there to find the quiet and beauty that they needed to cure themselves.

Hem was a strange suffering, quite different from a *mushkil*, or a problem. The woman who had a *mushkil* knew the reason for her pain. If she suffered from *hem*, however, she did not know what was wrong with her. Whatever was making her suffer had no name. Aunt Habiba said that you were lucky if you knew what hurt, because then you could do something about it. The woman who had *hem* could do nothing, except sit there silently, with her eyes wide open and her chin tucked into the palm of her hand, as if her neck could no longer hold up her head.

Because only quiet and beauty could cure women affected by *hem*, they were often taken to sanctuaries on the tops of high mountains, such as Moulay Abdesslam in the Rif, Moulay Bouazza in the Atlas, or one of the many retreats lying near the ocean between Tangier and Agadir. In our harem, we were lucky, because only Cousin Chama was sometimes affected by *hem*, and even she was not completely under its spell. Usually, she was stricken only when she listened to a special program on Radio Cairo about Huda Sha⁽raoui and the progress of women's rights in Egypt and Turkey. Then, *hem* would seize her. 'My

155

generation is being sacrificed!' she would cry. 'Revolution is liberating women in Turkey and Egypt, and we are left out here, up in the air. Neither part of the tradition, nor fully benefiting from modernity. Up hanging in the middle, like neglected butterflies.' Whenever Chama cried out like this, we would surround her with *hanan*, that unlimited, unrestricted tenderness, until she recovered. Silent, natural beauty and tenderness are the only medicines for that kind of disease.

The other woman in the house who sometimes secretly climbed up onto the forbidden terrace was Aunt Habiba. She had begun using the terrace when she first came to live with us, after her divorce. And it was from her that we learned how to get up there without using a ladder. We, the children, knew Aunt Habiba's secret because she needed us to watch the courtyard and the stairs when she was climbing up onto the forbidden terrace. She would take two of the gigantic laundry poles that were kept on the lower terrace (these were used for drying heavy wash like wool blankets and carpets, which were cleaned only in August, when the sun was the hottest) and use them like a ladder. It was not an easy operation. First, Aunt Habiba would stabilize the poles by putting them in empty olive jars, with cushions at the bottom to muffle the noise. Then, she would cross the two poles at the top, so as to create a step onto which she could place her foot. Beneath this step, she would create other steps with the wooden boxes lying around the terrace. The wooden boxes would get her three or even four meters above the ground, and then the final step, created by the poles, would allow her to push herself up onto the forbidden terrace. We would never have guessed how to do this without seeing Aunt Habiba in action.

The olive jars were as essential to the operation as were the poles. Black olives were brought to the house from the country-side in October, and at first, they were stored in huge bamboo containers with heaps of sea salt and stones on top, in order to press out the bitter juice. (Fresh olives are far too bitter to eat.) After their juices had been squeezed out, the olives would be removed from their bamboo containers, placed in big earthen jars, and left out on the terrace to be cured by the sun. From time to time, Aunt Habiba would expose the olives to the open air by spreading them flat on a sheet in a remote corner of the terrace, and once they were all wrinkled and cured, she would add heaps of fresh oregano and other herbs to them, and place them back safely in their jars. By the end of February, the olives could be eaten, and the team of women in charge of preparing breakfast that day would come up to get a good bucketful of them. Eating black olives with strong mint tea, *khli*ᶜ,[1] and fresh bread was a most common and delicious breakfast.

I loved breakfast, not only because of the salty olives, but also because of *ch-hiwat*, which were delicacies provided by the eccentrics among the courtyard population who wanted to eat other things besides the ones officially available at the communal tables. Since you could not eat in front of others without sharing, the *ch-hiwat* turned breakfasts into feasts. The eccentrics had to provide us all with their own favorite foods, and in large enough quantities to satisfy the entire household. Some provided turkey and duck eggs, others had cravings for eucalyptus-scented honey from the forests of the Kenitra region. Some loved doughnuts, and brought dozens to be democratically shared. The most appreciated of eccentrics, however, were those who brought strange fruits out of season, or salted cheese from the Rif, served in palm leaves.

But to get back to the olives. Although we children did love

---

[1] *Khli*ᶜ is a kind of Moroccan bacon made of beef, which is dried in the sunny months of July or August, and then cooked with olive oil and fat, perfumed with dried coriander and cumin. Like olives, *khli*ᶜ ought to last, if prepared properly, through the year.

eating them, even more delightful was the knowledge that the jars were gradually being emptied of their contents. We used the jars for all kinds of projects. Climbing up onto the forbidden terrace was just one of them. Playing hide-and-go-seek was another.

Samir and Malika's purpose, when they climbed up onto the highest terrace, was to push their investigation of harems further. On our first visit, though, we did not get very far. Once we recovered our normal breathing patterns, the beauty and quiet got ahold of us. We sat very still, watching and not wanting to move, because we were sitting so close together that the slightest motion annoyed the others. Even when I adjusted my braids, pinning them back up on top of my head, the other two complained. Then Malika asked a question, a rather simple question: 'Is a harem a house in which a man lives with many wives?' Each one of us came up with a different answer. Malika said the answer was yes, since that was the case with her own family. Her father, Uncle Karim, had two wives – her mother Biba and the co-wife Knata. Samir said the answer was no, because you could have a harem without co-wives, like that of his own father, Uncle ʿAli, or my father. (A fierce hatred of co-wives was just about the only thing that my mother and Lalla Radia, Samir's mother, had in common.)

My answer to Malika's question was more complicated. I said that it depended. If I thought about Grandmother Yasmina, the answer was yes. If I thought about Mother, the answer was no. But complicated answers make others resentful, because they make the confusion worse, and so both Samir and Malika ignored my contribution and kept arguing between themselves, while I drifted off and watched the clouds overhead, which seemed to be coming closer and closer. Finally, Samir and Malika decided that they had started with too complicated a question. We had to go back to the beginning, and ask the silliest question of all, 'Do all married men have harems?' From there, we could work our way up.

The three of us agreed that Ahmed the doorkeeper was married. He lived right by the gate in two tiny bedrooms with his wife Luza and their five children. But his house was not a harem. So it was not marriage that did it. Did that mean then, I said, that you could not have a harem if you were not a rich man? I felt very clever asking that question and it turned out to be a hell of a good one, because it kept both Malika and Samir silent for a while. Then Malika, who regularly abused her advantage of age, asked a lewd, indecent question that we did not expect: 'Maybe a man needs a big thing under his *djellaba* to create a harem, and Ahmed has only a small one?' Samir put an end to that line of inquiry immediately. He said that each one of us had an angel sitting on our right and left shoulders, who put down every word we said into a big book. On Judgment Day, that book was scrutinized, our deeds evaluated, and in the end, only the lucky ones who had nothing to be ashamed of were admitted to paradise. The others were thrown into hell. 'I don't want to be embarrassed,' concluded Samir. When we asked him where he had gotten this information, he said that it was from our teacher, Lalla Tam. At that, we decided that from now on, we would restrict our questioning to the *halal*, or the permissible, and I tried to put the possible mysterious link between the size of a man's sex and his right to a harem out of my mind.

The second time we climbed up onto the forbidden terrace, we were a lot more relaxed, both because its height seemed less frightening, and because we knew that we were going to stick with the *halal*. Our question this time was, 'Can you have more than one master in a harem?' It was a tough question, and one which kept us all silently engrossed in our own thoughts for some time. Then Samir said that you could in some cases; in others, you could not. He compared our harem to that of Uncle

Karim, Malika's father. In Malika's harem, there was only one master. In ours, there were two. Both Uncle ⁿAli and Father were masters, although Uncle was a little more of a master than Father, because he was the older, firstborn son. Still, both Uncle and Father made decisions, and did or did not grant you permission to do what you wanted. And as Yasmina said, having two masters was better than having just one, because if you could not get permission from one master, you always could turn to the other. In Malika's house, things were pretty grim when Uncle Karim did not grant permission (he either gave it, or he did not, with no room for confusion). When Malika wanted permission to come home with us after Koranic school and stay until sunset, she had to first beg her father for weeks. But he did not listen. He said that a little girl had to come directly home after school. Finally, Malika enlisted the help of Lalla Mani, Lalla Radia, and Aunt Habiba, and the women only succeeded in making him change his mind by arguing that her uncle's house was identical to her father's, and that besides, she had no one her own age to play with at home. All her brothers and sisters were much older than she.

The more masters one had, the more freedom and the more fun. That was also the case at Yasmina's farm. Grandfather Tazi was the supreme authority, of course, but two of his eldest sons, Hadj Salem and Hadj Jalil, made decisions as well. When Grandfather was absent, they acted as his caliphs, often doing everything they could to aggravate Yasmina and the other co-wives. Yasmina would often aggravate them right back by claiming, for example, that Grandfather had granted her permission to go fishing before he left that morning at dawn, a statement which the two sons could not possibly disprove because they did not wake up before 8 A.M. Yasmina was always getting away with murder just because she woke up early, and she told me that if I wanted to be happy in life, I would have to wake up just before the birds, too. Then, she said, my life would unfold before me like a garden. The music of the little creatures would stir happiness within me, while I sat quietly reflecting on how to use my day and take the next small step forward. To be happy, she said, a woman had to think hard, during long silent hours, about how to make each small step forward. 'Figuring out who has *sulta* (authority) over you is the first step,' said Yasmina. 'That information is basic. But after that, you need to shuffle the cards, confuse the roles. That is the interesting part. Life is a game. Look at it that way, and you can laugh at the whole thing.' *Sulta*, authority, games. These were key words which kept popping up, and it struck me that maybe the harem itself was just a game. A game between men and women who were afraid of each other, and therefore always trying to prove how strong they were, just like we kids always did. But I could not share that thought that afternoon with Malika and Samir, for it sounded too crazy. It meant that grownups were no different than children.

When we left the terrace that day, we were so engrossed in our inquiry that we did not even notice the pink clouds drifting silently toward the west, nor much of anything else. We had not found any answers – in fact, we were more confused than ever, and we rushed to Aunt Habiba to ask for help. We found her absorbed in her embroidery, her head bent over her *mrema*, a horizontal wooden frame used for elaborate projects. The *mrema* resembled the men's large weaving loom, but was much smaller and lighter. A woman fitted the fabric tightly around, so it remained taut when the needle went through. The *mrema* was a very personal item, with each woman adjusting hers so she did not have to bend her head too much. Embroidery was primarily a solitary endeavor, but the women often teamed up together when they wanted to talk or when they were involved in a project that required a lot of work.

161

That day, Aunt Habiba was stitching a green bird with golden wings all by herself. Big birds stretching out their aggressive wings were not a classical design, and if Lalla Mani had seen it, she would have said that it was an awful innovation, and one that meant its creator had flight and escape on her mind. Of course, birds appeared in traditional embroidery designs, but they were tiny, and often totally paralyzed, squeezed as they were between gigantic plants and fat leafy flowers. Because of Lalla Mani's attitude, Aunt Habiba always embroidered classical designs when down in the courtyard, and kept her big, winged birds to herself, up in her private room, with its direct access to the lower terrace. I loved her so much. She was so silent, so apparently quiescent to the demands of a tough outside world, and yet, she still managed to hang onto her wings. She reassured me about the future: a woman could be totally powerless, and still give meaning to her life by dreaming about flight.

Malika, Samir, and I waited for Aunt Habiba to raise her head, and then we explained our problem and how we got confused every time we tried to clarify the harem business. After listening carefully, she said that we were stuck in a *tanaqod*, or contradiction. Being caught in a *tanaqod* meant that when you asked a question, you got too many answers, which only increased your confusion. 'And the problem with confusion,' Aunt Habiba said, 'is that you don't feel smart.' However, she went on, to become a grownup, you had to learn how to deal with *tanaqod*. The first step for beginners was to develop patience. You had to learn to accept that, for a while, whenever you asked a question, your confusion would only get worse. That was no reason, however, for a human being to stop using the most precious gift that Allah had bestowed upon us – *ʿaql*, or reason. 'And remember,' Aunt Habiba added, 'no one, up to now, has figured out a way to understand things without asking questions.'

Aunt Habiba also said something about time and space, about

how harems change from one part of the world to another, and from one century to the next. The harem kept by the Abbasid Caliph Harun al-Rashid in ninth-century Baghdad had nothing to do with our own. His *jaryas*, or slave girls, were very educated women, swallowing history and religious books as fast as they could, in order to entertain him. Men of that time did not appreciate the company of illiterate, uneducated women, and you had no chance of capturing the Caliph's attention if you could not dazzle him with your knowledge of science, history, and geography, not to mention jurisprudence. These subjects were the Caliph's obsession, and he spent most of his free time discussing them, between the two *jihads*, or holy wars. However, Aunt Habiba added, the Abbasid caliphs had lived a long time ago. Now, our harems were filled with illiterate women, which only went to show how far we had strayed from tradition. And as for power and might, the Arab leaders were no longer conquerors, they were the conquered, crushed by the colonial armies. Back when the *jaryas* had been super-educated, the Arab men had been on the top of the world. Now, both the men and the women were at the bottom, and the craving for education is a sign that we are emerging from our colonial humiliation. As Aunt Habiba was talking, I looked at Samir to see whether he understood everything she was saying. But he looked puzzled, too. Aunt Habiba noticed our restlessness and said not to worry, we need not get into time and space yet. What was important now was that we were advancing, even if we did not know it. For the moment, all we could do was go on with the mission.

A week later, during our next session on the forbidden terrace, Malika brought up the question of slaves. Did you need to have slaves to have a harem? Samir said that it was foolish to even ask such a thing, since we did not have any slaves in our harem. But Malika swiftly replied that there was Mina, who lived with us, and who was a slave. Samir retorted that Mina's presence among us was accidental. She had no husband, no children, and no relatives, and was with us because she belonged to no one and had nowhere to go. She was *maqtuᶜa,* cut off from her roots, like a dead tree. Years before, Mina had been kidnapped from her native Sudan, somewhere south of the Sahara, and sold as a slave in Marrakech. Then she had been sold in one slave market after the next, until she ended up in our house as a cook. Soon after that, she asked Uncle ᶜAli to exempt her from housework because she wanted to retire to the rooftop and pray. There was too much noise and talk down in the courtyard. And so, with the exception of the winter months, when the cold winds came down from the land of the Christians, Mina would camp on the lower terrace, facing Mecca.

17

Mina, The Rootless

Mina camped on the lower terrace, facing Mecca, and was seated on an ageless sheepskin with a saffron-colored leather cushion from Mauritania supporting her back as she leaned against the western wall. Saffron was her color. Both her headdress and her caftan were golden yellow, and they gave her serene black face an unusual glow. She was condemned to wear yellow because she was possessed by a foreign *djinni* who forbade her to wear other colors. The *djinnis* were terribly willful spirits who would get ahold of people and make them follow their caprices, like wearing specific colors, or dancing to particular music, even in countries where dancing by women was considered improper. Traditionally, a respectable adult wore discreet colors and rarely danced, and never in public. Only bad or half-crazy, possessed men and women danced in public, said Lalla Mani, a statement which always amazed Mother. She would retort by saying that most of rural Morocco danced happily away during religious festivals, with long lines of men, women, and children holding hands and jumping up and down until morning. And these same people still managed to produce enough food to feed us. 'I thought that crazy people didn't do their work correctly,' Mother would taunt, while Lalla Mani argued right back that when you were possessed by a *djinni*, you lost all sense of the *hudud*, or the frontier between good and bad, between *haram* and *halal*. 'Women possessed by the *djinnis* leap high in the air when they hear their rhythm playing,' she said, 'and they shake their bodies shamelessly, with hands and legs flying over their heads.'

Mina remembered fragments of her native language from her childhood, but they were mostly songs which did not make any sense either to her or to anyone else. Sometimes, too, Mina was sure that the *djinni* drum music, played during the *hadra*, or dance possession rituals, was reminiscent of the rhythms she had known in childhood. Other times, she was not so sure. She could describe trees, fruits, and animals, however, that no one ever had seen in Fez. We would sometimes encounter these in Aunt Habiba's stories, especially when we crossed the desert with a caravan going to Timbuktu, and then, Mina would ask Aunt Habiba to elaborate. Aunt Habiba, who was illiterate, and who had gotten her information by listening carefully when her husband had read out loud from history and literature, would call Chama to her rescue. Chama would then rush upstairs and bring back reference books written by Arab geographers. She would look up Timbuktu in the index and read pages and pages out loud, so Mina might get a feel for her childhood. Mina would sit quietly listening throughout, although sometimes she would ask for a passage to be read many times, especially if it was a description of a marketplace, or a neighborhood. 'I might run into someone I know,' she would joke, with one hand in front of her mouth, hiding her shy smile. 'I might run into my sister or brother. Or I might be recognized by a friend from childhood.' She would then excuse herself for interrupting the tale. Mina was *maqtuᶜa*, old and poor, but she gave much warmth and *hanan*. *Hanan* is such a divine gift, it bubbles up like a fountain, splashing tenderness all around, regardless of whether or not its receiver is well behaved and careful not to stray outside Allah's *hudud*. Only saints and other privileged creatures provided *hanan*, and Mina had it. She never showed any anger, except when a child was beaten.

Mina danced once a year, during the Mouloud festival, the anniversary of the birth of the Prophet, Peace and Allah's Prayers be Upon Him. At that time, many, many rituals took place all over the city, from the most official, but wonderful, all-male religious choruses held in the magnificent Moulay Driss' sanctuary, to the ambiguous *hadra*, or possession dances, which took place in the neighborhoods. Mina participated in the ritual organized at the house of Sidi Belal, the most renowned and effective of the *djinni* exorcists in the entire Fez region. Like Mina, he had originally come from the Sudan and begun his life in Morocco as an uprooted slave. But he was so good at taming the *djinnis*, that his owners went into business with him. Not just anyone could attend the ceremonies in Sidi Belal's house, either. You needed an invitation.

The *djinnis* possessed slaves as well as the freeborn, and men as well as women. However, the *djinnis* seemed to recruit more easily among the powerless and the poor, and the poor were their most reliable devotees. 'For the rich, the *hadra* is more of an amusement,' explained Mina, 'while for women like me, it is a rare opportunity to get away, to exist in a different way, to travel.' For a businessman like Sidi Belal, of course, the rare attendance of women from high-ranking families was absolutely vital, and they came to his house, bearing expensive gifts. Their presence and generosity were appreciated by all as an expression of women's solidarity, and their support was much needed. The nationalists were against possession dances, declaring them to be against Islam and *shariʿa*, or religious law. And since all the heads of distinguished families shared the nationalists' views, women attended Sidi Belal's *hadra* in total secrecy. Mina also attended the *hadra* in secrecy because Father and Uncle agreed wholeheartedly with the nationalists, but all the women and the children in the house knew about it anyway, and practically all of us had accompanied her. You always needed a friend to accompany you to a possession dance, because after hours of jumping and singing, you often fainted with fatigue. Since Mina was so popular, all the courtyard declared itself to be her friend. But indeed, beyond friendship, we all were irresistibly drawn to the evidently subversive possession ceremony, during which women would dance away with their eyes closed and their long hair floating from left and right, as if all modesty and bodily constraints had been abandoned. Even we children would manage to get there, by threatening to tell Father and Uncle all about it. Blackmailing the adult women gave us a lot of power, and assured our right to participate in practically every forbidden ceremony.

Sidi Belal's house was as big as ours, although it did not have our luxurious marble floors and lavish woodwork. The *hadra* would begin with hundreds of women, all elaborately dressed and made up, lined up in orderly fashion on sofas along the courtyard's four walls. Sitting arm in arm, the women would be clustered around their *meriaha*, or the woman who could not resist the *rih*, the rhythm which compelled her to dance. Sidi Belal himself would be standing in the middle of the courtyard, in a flowing green robe and saffron turban and slippers, surrounded by an all-male orchestra made up of drums, *guenbris* (lute-like instruments), and cymbals.

The four rooms around the courtyard would be occupied by women from the richest families, those who had brought the most expensive gifts and did not want to be seen dancing, while the poorer women sat in the courtyard. Precious silver tea trays, with multi-colored Bohemian crystal glasses, and bronze samovars sizzling with steaming hot water, would be prepared in the four corners of the courtyard and in the middle of each salon. Then, we would be requested to not move anymore. The essential rule, valid for all ceremonies, religious or profane, was that everyone find a place and remain still, which was why we children were barely tolerated. Since there were usually ten of us children who snuck in with Mina, Aunt Habiba had instituted a simple but inflexible rule: each child could select someone to sit close to, but if we stood up, started running around, tried to talk to other children, or refused to sit back down after the third warning, we were shown to the door. I had no trouble with that rule, so passive and tranquil was I, but poor Samir never made it to the end of the ceremony. He could not sit still for five minutes in a row. Once, he even shouted insults at Sidi Belal as he was escorted by Aunt Habiba to the door. The following year, she had to fabricate a little turban to hide his locks, so that the master of ceremonies would not recognize him.

At first, Sidi Belal's orchestra would play slowly, so slowly that the women would keep on talking to one another as if nothing was happening. But then, suddenly, the drums would beat out a strange rhythm, and all the *meriahat* would spring up, toss away their headgear and slippers, bend from the waist, and swing their long hair wildly about. As their necks swung from side to side, they also seemed to lengthen, as if trying to escape from whatever was squeezing them. Sometimes Sidi Belal, frightened by the violence of the dancers' movements and afraid that they might hurt themselves, would gesture to his orchestra to slow down. But often, by then, it was too late, and the women would ignore the music and carry on at their own impetuous speed, as if to indicate that the master of ceremonies no longer controlled anything. It was as if the women had freed themselves for once of all external pressures. Many would have light smiles floating on their faces, and with their half-closed eyes, they sometimes gave the impression that they were emerging from an enchanting dream. At the end of the ceremony, the women would collapse onto the floor, totally exhausted and half unconscious. Then, their friends would hug them, congratulate them, throw rosewater in their faces, and whisper secret things in their ears. Slowly, the dancers would recover and return to their places as if nothing had happened.

Mina danced slowly with her head swaying just slightly from right to left and her body erect. She only reacted to the softest of the rhythms, and even then, she danced off of the beat, as if the music she was dancing to was coming from inside. I admired her for that and for a reason I still do not understand. Maybe it was because I always enjoyed slow motion, and dreamed of life as a quiet and unhurried dance. Or maybe it was because Mina managed to combine two seemingly contradictory roles – to dance with a group, but also to keep her own offbeat rhythm. I wanted to dance like her, with the community, but also to my own secret music, springing from a mysterious source deep within, and stronger than the drums. Stronger, and yet softer and more liberating. Once I asked Mina why she danced so smoothly while most of the other women made abrupt, jerky movements, and she said that many of the women confused liberation with agitation. 'Some ladies are angry with their lives,' she said 'and so even their dance becomes an expression of that.' Angry women are hostages of their anger. They cannot escape it and set themselves free, which is indeed a sad fate. The worst of prisons is the self-created one.

According to legend, the all-male orchestra at the *hadra* ritual was supposed to be all black. These musicians, said the legend, had come from a fabulous empire called Gnawa (Ghana), which stretched beyond the Sahara Desert, and beyond the rivers, all the way down south, into the heart of the Sudan. When they had come north, they had brought with them no luggage but their enchanting, irresistible rhythms and songs, and their preferred city in Morocco was Marrakech, the open door to the desert.

Everyone said that Marrakech, also known as Al-Hamra, or the Red-Walled City, had nothing in common with Fez, which was located too near the Christian frontier and the Mediterranean, and was swept by too many bitter cold winter winds. Marrakech, on the other hand, was deeply tuned to the African currents, and we heard many wondrous things about what it was like. Not many in our courtyard had seen Marrakech, but everyone knew one or two mysterious things about it.

The walls were flaming red in Marrakech, and so was the earth you walked on. Marrakech was blazing hot, and yet there was nearly always snow up above it, shining on the Atlas Mountains. In ancient times, you see, Atlas had been a Greek god living in the Mediterranean Sea. He was a Titan fighting against other giants, and one day he lost an important battle. So he came to hide on the African shores, and when he lay down to sleep, he tucked his head into Tunisia and stretched his feet as far as Marrakech. The 'bed' was so nice that he never woke up again, and became a mountain. Snow visited Atlas regularly each year for months, and he seemed to be enchanted to feel his feet trapped in the desert, and twinkled to passersby from his royal captivity.

Marrakech was the city where black and white legends met, languages melted down, and religions stumbled, testing their permanence against the undisturbed silence of the dancing sands. Marrakech was the unsettling place where pious pilgrims discovered that the body was a god too, and that all the rest, including reason and the soul, and all their authoritarian priests and earnest executioners, could fade and disappear when the drums slit the air. People danced in Marrakech, travelers said, when their differing languages did not allow them to communicate. I liked the idea of a city engrossed in dancing, when words failed to create links. That was what happened in Sidi Belal's courtyard, I thought, when the women, renewed with the strengths of those ancient civilizations, danced out all their invincible desires. The *djinnis* came from faraway alien territories, entered entrapped bodies, and started speaking foreign languages to them.

Sometimes, someone would spot a white drummer in Sidi Belal's supposedly all-Gnawa black orchestra, and then the honorable ladies who had paid for the ceremony would complain. 'How can you perform Gnawa music, and sing genuine Gnawa songs, when you are white like an aspirin tablet!' they would shout, furious at the lousy organization. Sidi Belal would try to explain to them that sometimes, even if you were white, Gnawa culture could rub off on you and you could learn its music and songs. But the women were adamant – the orchestra had to be all black and foreign. The blacks in the orchestra had better speak Arabic with an accent too, otherwise they might be nothing more than local blacks who could play drums. Thanks to centuries of travel and trade across the desert, there were hundreds of local blacks living in the Fez Medina who could have posed as distinguished foreign visitors from the prestigious Empire of Ghana. Local blacks simply would not do, either, because even if they could fool the women, they surely could not fool the foreign *djinnis*. And that would have defeated the entire ceremony's goal, which was to communicate with the *djinnis* in their mysterious languages. Was not the dance a leap into alien worlds? In any case, too, the women preferred having a genuine Gnawa orchestra, because they did not appreciate the idea of some local guy from the Medina ogling them while they were absorbed in their dances. They preferred to perform in front of strangers, who knew nothing of the city's laws and codes. It was therefore lucky for all concerned that Sidi Belal's orchestra usually kept silent when not playing, so that the question of accent did not often arise.

Despite all the excitement surrounding the annual ceremony at Sidi Belal's house, most of the time Mina's life flowed by unnoticed. She shared a tiny room on the top floors with three other elderly slave women – Dada Saʿada, Dada Rahma, and Aishata. All had already been living in the house long before even Samir's mother and mine had moved in. Like Mina, they did not have any clear relationship to the family, but had drifted in when the ban on slavery was enforced by the French. 'It was only when the French made it possible for the slaves to file suits in courts to recover their freedom,' Mina would say, 'and when the slave traders were given prison sentences and fines, that slavery finally stopped. Only when the court steps in does violence end.'[1]

---

[1] Mina probably was referring to the 1922 Circulaire de l'Administration Française, which went beyond making the public sale of slaves illegal (it had already been so for decades in Morocco), by giving the victims – the slaves themselves – the opportunity to free themselves by suing their abductors and buyers in court. Shortly after implementation of the Circulaire, slavery died out in Morocco. This accomplishment stood in stark contrast to the fact that for decades after the formal international ban on slavery, Arab officials resisted it. Only when women get the law on their side, and can easily sue their aggressors, does change occur.

Just as women's rights are rejected in Muslim countries today as a form of Western aggression against Muslim values, the ban on slavery promoted by the colonial powers was opposed and decried by many Arab rulers throughout the nineteenth and early twentieth centuries as a violation of Islam. Many Muslim officials and spokespersons for members of the ruling class, who still bought or sold slaves, opposed the ban as yet another example of colonial arrogance.

However, actually, one of the achievements of early Islam was its bold anti-slavery stance. The Prophet Mohammed encouraged his believers in seventh-century Medina to free their slaves, as he himself had freed his, even giving his famous slave Bilal and Bilal's son, Ousama, key positions

Once freed, however, many female slaves like Mina were too weak to fight, too shy to seduce, too breathless to protest, and too poor to return to their native lands. Or else, they were too unsure of what they would find once they were back there. All they really wanted was a calm room to stretch out in and let the years roll by. A place where they could forget about the senseless succession of days and nights, and dream of a better world in which violence and women walked separate paths. But while Dada Saᶜada, Dada Rahma, Aishata, and most of the other female relatives who lived on the top floors kept to their rooms, Mina thrived on the terrace. Since she never divulged any secrets (and in fact, hardly talked at all, except with us children), her presence did not inconvenience anyone either. Not the young men sneaking up there to catch a glimpse of the girls next door; not the women climbing up to burn magic candles, or, even worse, to smoke sinful, very-rare-to-find American cigarettes stolen out of Zin's or Jawad's pockets; and not the children hiding in the forbidden olive jars.

Those jars were my own secret addiction, and my morbid fascination with them disturbed many, and precipitated a high-level family council meeting. I never confessed though, when Grandmother Lalla Mani, acting as chairperson, asked me why I felt the gruesome need to slide down into those huge, dark, empty olive jars. I never said that it had to do with Mina's kidnapping, for if I had, she would have been blamed. Mina was incredibly popular with us children, so much so that mothers

of power. But that historical heritage did not influence the position of some of the conservative Arab leaders who resisted the slavery ban by camouflaging it as an attack on the *umma*, the Muslim community, which is exactly what they are doing today with women's rights. They know too well that they cannot promote democracy without liberating women. Their resistance to women's rights is in fact a rejection of democratic principles and human rights.

would enlist her help when they were having a hard time communicating with their sons or daughters. I loved her very much, and did not want her to get in trouble, especially since she had already had so much trouble when she was a child barely my age. For you see, she was kidnapped one day when she was strolling just a bit farther than usual from her parents' house. A big hand seized her and the the next thing she knew, she was on the road, along with other children, and two ferocious kidnappers brandishing long knives.

Mina remembered, only too well, the way it all happened – the way the kidnappers kept her and all the other children hidden during the day, and the way they moved them at dusk when the sun set. Crossing her beloved familiar forest, they traveled far north until there was no more vegetation, just dunes of white sands. 'If you've never seen the Sahara Desert before,' Mina said, 'you cannot imagine it. That's where you see how powerful Allah is – he definitely does not need us! A human life is so negligible in the desert, where only sand dunes and stars can survive. A little girl's pain there is an utter trifle. But it was in crossing the sand that I discovered there was another little girl inside me. A girl who was strong, and intent on surviving. I became a different Mina then. I realized that all the world was set against me, and the only good that I could expect had to come from inside myself.'

Her black kidnappers, who spoke her native language, were soon replaced by light-skinned ones, who spoke foreign words that she did not understand.[2] 'Before, I thought the entire planet

---

[2] Local slave traders handed their victims over to Arab slave traders, who then continued traveling along customary trade routes towards the North. See the maps in E. W. Bovill's *The Golden Trade of the Moors* (Oxford University Press, 1970), specifically chap. 25, 'The Last Caravans,' p. 236 and 239.

spoke our dialect,' Mina said. The party traveled silently by night and was met regularly at specific, pre-arranged spots by friends of the kidnappers who fed them and kept them hidden until the next sunset. They always would start marching when the sands disappeared in the dark, and hardly a creature ever crossed their path. The French outposts, scattered here and there in the occupied desert, were to be avoided at any cost, for the slave trade had already been declared illegal.

One day, they crossed a river, and Mina, for some strange reason, thought that she saw her beloved old forest appearing at the horizon. She asked another little girl who had been stolen from her village if she also saw the forest, and the girl nodded yes. They both believed that, by a magic turn of events, their kidnappers had gotten lost, and they were going back home. Or else their village was coming towards them. Either way, it did not matter, and that night the two little girls ran away, only to be caught again a few hours later. 'One has to be careful in life,' Mina would say, 'not to confuse wishes with reality. But we did, and we paid for it.'

When Mina reached this point in her story, her voice would quiver, and everyone around her would cry out in distress, especially when she went into the details. 'They detached the well bucket from its rope,' she said, 'and told me that if I wanted to stay alive, I had to hang onto the end of that rope and concentrate in silence, while they lowered me into the dark well. The horrible thing was that I could not even afford to tremble with fear, because if I did, the rope would slip out of my fingers. It would be the end.' Mina would stop there and sob softly. Then she would dry her tears, and keep on going with the audience crying discreetly. 'I cry now,' she would say, 'because I am still so angry that they did not give me a chance to be afraid. I knew that I would soon reach the deepest and darkest part of the well, where water was, but I had to suppress that terrified feeling. I had to! Or else I would lose my grip, and so I kept concentrating on the rope and my fingers around it. There was another little girl beside me, another Mina who was dissolving with fear as her body was about to touch the cold, dark water filled with snakes and slippery things, but I had to disassociate myself from her so as to concentrate on the rope. When they took me out of that well, I was blind for days, not because I could not see, but because I was not interested in looking at the world anymore.'

Tales of abductions by slave traders were common in *A Thousand and One Nights*, where many of the heroines who began life as princesses were kidnapped and sold as slaves when their royal caravans, heading towards Mecca for the pilgrimage, were attacked.[3] None of these tales had the same effect on me, though, as Mina's description of her descent into the well. I had nightmares when I first heard it, but never told Mother what had frightened me when she came in to hug me and bring me into her bed. She and Father would hold me tight, and kiss me, and try to figure out what was the matter, and why I could not go to sleep. But I did not tell them about the well, for fear that they would prevent me from hearing Mina's story again. And I needed to hear that story told again, and again, and again, so that I, too, could cross the desert and arrive safely at the terrace. Talking to Mina was essential, because I needed to know all the details. I needed to know more – I needed to know how to get out of the well.

You see, not everyone in our house agreed on what children should or should not hear. Many family members, like Lalla Mani, thought that it was disastrous for children to hear about

---

[3] One of the most famous is the abduction of Princess Nuzhatu al-Zaman, in 'The Tale of King Omar Bin al-Nu'man and his Sons' (Burton translation, vol.2). The abduction starts on page 141 and is very similar to Mina's.

violence. Others said that the sooner we learned about it, the better. Those in the second camp said that it was essential to teach a child how to protect himself or herself, how to escape, how to avoid being paralyzed by fear. Mina belonged to the second camp. 'Going into that well,' she would say, 'made me see that when you are in trouble, you need to put all your energies into thinking that there is a way out. Then, the bottom, the dark hole, becomes just a springboard from which you can leap so high that your head might hit a cloud. You see what I mean?'

> *Yes Mina, I thought, I see what you mean, I see it so well. I just need to learn how to jump up so high as to reach the clouds.*
> *I will learn the lifesaving leaps by sliding down into the olive jars, to train and be ready for the big scares to come.*
> *I will learn how to shine like you do, in spite of it all, with your back to the western wall, facing Mecca, and with* hanan, *that ever-flowing tenderness.*
> *'I am sure that Mecca knows all about the well and the kidnappers, don't you Mina?' I said to her one day, 'Allah must have punished all those who hurt you. Allah must have done it, and I don't ever have to be afraid, do I?'*

Mina was very optimistic and said that no, there was no reason at all why I should be afraid. 'Life is looking good for women now,' she said, 'with the nationalists asking for their education, and the end of seclusion. For you know, the problem with women today is that they are powerless. And powerlessness stems from ignorance and a lack of education. You are going to be a powerful women, aren't you? I would be so upset if you weren't. Just concentrate on that little circle of sky hanging above the well. There is always a little part of the sky you can raise your head to. So, don't look down, look up, up, and off we go! Making wings!'

After provoking Mina into telling me the story of her escape from the well over and over again, and by sliding down myself, more or less regularly, into the dark olive jar, I forgot all about my fears, and my nightmare disappeared. I discovered that I was a magic creature. I just needed to fix my sights on the sky, aim high, and everything would be all right. Even when they are tiny, little girls can surprise monsters. In fact, what fascinated me about Mina's story was how she surprised her kidnappers: they expected her to scream and she did not. I thought that was so clever and told Mina that I could surprise a monster too, if I had to. Yes, Mina said, but you need to know him very well first. She had observed her kidnappers for a long time, for the trip had taken weeks.

Mina said that you always had a choice, when stuck in a pit, between pleasing the monster by looking down and screaming, or surprising him by looking up. If you wanted to please him, you looked down, and thought about all the snakes and other cold, slow-moving creatures crawling around on top of each other down there and waiting to get ahold of you. If, on the other hand, you wished to astonish the monster, you fixed your eyes up high on that little drop of sky and avoided uttering a sound. Then, the torturer who was watching you from above would see your eyes and get scared. 'He'll think you are either a *djinni*, or two little stars twinkling in the dark.'

The idea of Mina, the tiny Mina, that scared little thing, lost in the sand with strangers, transforming herself into two twinkling stars, was an idea that I never forgot. It was a vision which haunted me then and still haunts me today, and every time I manage to find the silence required to visualize it, energy and hope spring from within. But I needed to train myself to get out of the well first, and for a while, jumping into dark, empty olive jars became my favorite game. I could only indulge in it, however, when a grownup was around, because Samir thought it was too dangerous for a children's game.

I was so happy every time Mina helped me get out of the well that I would obsessively put myself into one by sliding down into a huge, dark, empty olive jar. We children used the jars to play hide-and-go-seek either by making ourselves invisible behind them or, when we really wanted to hug fear close, by sliding down into one. But you ran the danger, when sliding down, of getting stuck. A grownup's help would then be necessary. Mina, who practically lived on the terrace, with her back to the western wall, would watch us play our morbid game in silence, waiting for the next catastrophe to occur. Then, when you started screaming for help, she would stand up and come over to peep down at you. 'Can't you wait for fear to chase after you,' she would say, 'instead of rushing out to meet it? Now keep still, and don't panic. I will get you out in a minute.' So then you just had to relax and try to breathe normally, with your eyes focused on the tiny circle of blue sky up above. Soon, you heard the sounds of feet shuffling on the terrace floor, and Mina's voice whispering rescue instructions to Dada Sa'ada, Dada Rahma, and Aishata. Next, there would be a mini-earthquake, the jar would be tilted horizontally, and you would crawl out.

Every time Mina helped me out, I would jump at her neck and hug her enthusiastically. 'Don't hug me so tight, you're messing up my headgear,' she would say. 'And what would have happened if I was in the bathroom or involved in my prayers? Hum?' Then, I would tuck my head into her neck and swear never to get stuck in an olive jar again. Once I saw that she was mellowing and letting me play with the ends of her turban, I would venture to ask a favor. 'Mina, can I sit on your lap, and listen to how you escaped from the well?'

'But I have told you about that a hundred times! What's the matter with you? You already know all the essentials: a little girl, as small as she is, has enough energy inside her to defy torturers, to be courageous and patient, and to waste no time trembling and screaming. I told you that the kidnapper expected me to cry and scream. But when he heard no sound, and saw two twinkling stars fixed on him, he immediately brought me back up. He did not expect defiant silence and a calm stare. He expected me to howl. But you already knew all that!' Then I would swear that this was the last time I would need the story repeated, and I was finished with the jars forever.

Until the next time.

18

American Cigarettes

Fooling around with olive jars was not the only illegal activity that took place on the terrace. Grownups committed worse crimes, such as chewing gum, putting on red fingernail polish, and smoking cigarettes, although these last two activities took place rarely, given the difficulty of obtaining such foreign items in the first place. More common crimes were the burning of charmed candles to create the allure of *qbul* (sex appeal), the bobbing of hair with bangs to look like the French actress Claudette Colbert, or the plotting of escapes to the outside world so as to attend the nationalist meetings taking place at someone's house or at the Qaraouiyine Mosque. Since we children could have gotten any of the adult criminals in trouble with Father, Uncle, and Lalla Mani if we described what we saw, we were treated with exceptional indulgence, and enjoyed an unusually comfortable position on the terrace. No grownup could boss us around without us threatening to retaliate by informing the authorities. And indeed, the authorities relied heavily on us when they suspected something fishy was going on, for they believed that 'children tell the truth.' All the trespassers, therefore, gave us VIP treatment, showering us with cookies, roasted almonds, and *sfinge* (doughnuts), and never forgetting to hand us our tea before everyone else.

Mina watched all this in silence, redoubling her prayers to save everyone's soul. What she objected to the most, was when the young men of the house came up to the terrace to look at the Bennis girls. That, she thought, was something utterly sinful, a dangerous violation of the *hudud*, or sacred frontiers. It was true that the youth of each house kept to its own terrace, but they often sang love songs that were loud enough to be heard by their neighbors. Chama danced also, and so did the Bennis girls, thus managing to sculpt fleeting moments when adolescent love and happiness floated around, and turned the sunset into a red and romantic haze. Worst of all for Mina, though, was the fact that the boys and girls did not just look at each other from the terrace – they exchanged love glances.

A love glance was when you looked at a man with your eyelids half closed, as if you were about to go to sleep. Chama was wonderful at it, and was already receiving numerous marriage proposals from promising sons of distinguished nationalist families, who had caught a glimpse of her while she was singing 'Maghribuna watanuna' (Our Morocco, Our Homeland) during street demonstrations or during the Qaraouiyine Mosque celebrations when political prisoners were released by the French. Malika said she would consider teaching me how to do the love glance, if I promised to give her a substantial portion of my cookies, almonds, and *sfinge*. Malika herself already was getting a lot of attention from the boys at the Koranic school, and I was eager to know her secret. Finally she said vaguely, when I pressed her, that she used a combination of the love glance and the mental recitation of a *qbul* formula, gotten from a medieval charm book, which was supposed to captivate forever the heart of the men whose love you wanted.[1] I was extremely interested in the whole thing and tried to get Samir interested, too, by secretly 'borrowing' one of Chama's books, but he complained that I was getting too involved in this new beauty and love business, and was neglecting all our other projects and games. I realized then that Malika represented my only chance to get the vital information I wanted about beauty and sex appeal, which were becoming more and more interesting every day. However, I did not want to give her the impression that I was desperate, and so I told her I needed to think it over before deciding about the cookies.

The grownups on the terrace always treated Samir and me as if we did not know anything about love and babies. They also treated us as if we did not know how important it was to make yourself beautiful so as to attract the love of the opposite sex. Malika also told us a few times that love was far from being a simple matter, and I listened carefully as she outlined the intricacies, all the while wondering if she was not just pressuring me about the cookie deal. She said that the most difficult thing about the whole business was not making someone fall in love with you, but keeping that love alive. For love has wings – it

---

[1] What I call here a 'charm book' is part of an important Arabic literary genre, concerned with *chifa*, or cures, which flourished from medieval times to the nineteenth century. On the fringe of Arab medical thought, it combined scientific medical chapters on the one hand (often at the beginning of the book) with highly amusing magic recipes and formulas from beauty masks and sex-appeal treatments, to birth control methods, aphrodisiac concoctions, and cures for impotence. These books are still very popular. Available in the traditional city street-vendors' stalls, they are utterly fascinating for a child because of their symbolic talisman charts and the beautiful calligraphy of their magic formulas.

For more information, see chapter 19, page 201, note 1.

comes and goes. I decided then that for the moment I would simplify things and concentrate on the initial seduction; I could deal later with the problem of making love last forever.

A woman needed to do two things in order to capture a man's love. One was magic. She had to burn a candle during the full moon and chant an incantation that all girls learned at some point or another. The second was a complicated process that took forever: she had to make herself beautiful. She had to take care of her hair, her skin, her hands, her legs, and . . . Oh, I am sure I have forgotten something. Anyway, Aunt Habiba said that there was no rush; I had plenty of time to learn about beauty techniques.

I already knew what to do in order to have beautiful hair, for Mother had decided that mine was dreadful. It was curly and unruly, and I had more of it than was considered becoming for a young girl. So once a week, Mother would put two or three fresh tobacco leaves, smuggled in at great expense from the Rif Mountains where it grew in large fields, into half a cup of boiling olive oil. (Dried tobacco for sniffing would do when you could not get fresh leaves.) She let the boiling oil sit for a while, with the tobacco in it, and then patiently parted my hair into fine strands and rubbed in the oil. Next, she braided my hair and fastened it to the top of my head so as not to dirty my clothes, and I had to avoid hugging or kissing anyone until it was time to go to the *hammam*, or communal bath. There, Mother diluted henna in hot water and rubbed it all over my hair, before washing everything away. Mother said that you couldn't expect much of a woman who did not take care of her hair, and I wanted people to expect a lot of me.

The washing-away part was what I enjoyed the most, for going to the *hammam* was like stepping onto a warm, misty island. I would borrow Mother's precious Turkish silver bowl, sit on her Syrian wood and mother-of-pearl stool, and wash my hair the way she did. I would use the bowl to take the water from the bucket of warm water from the gigantic fountain, and pour the water all over my head. I only stopped when Mother heard other people screaming that the henna was splashing all over the place, and into my immediate neighbors' eyes. But I would always leave the *hammam* without paying any attention to my detractors, and walk away feeling as beautiful as Princess Budur.

Visiting our neighborhood *hammam*, with its white marble floors and glass ceiling, was such a delight, I decided one day as I was splashing about, that I definitely would find a way to take one – along with my beloved terrace – with me wherever I went as an adult. The *hammam* and the terrace were the two most pleasurable aspects of harem life, Mother said, and the only things worth keeping. She wanted me to study hard to get a diploma and become someone important, and to build a house for myself with a *hammam* on the first floor, and a terrace on the second. I wondered then where I would live and sleep, and she said 'But on the terrace, dear! You can get a removable glass ceiling to use when you are going to sleep, or when it is cold. With all these new things now being invented by the Christians, by the time you grow up, you'll be able to buy glass houses with removable ceilings.' From the harem, the possibilities to make life enjoyable seemed infinite – walls were going to disappear, and houses with glass ceilings were going to replace them. Imprisoned behind walls, women walked around dreaming of frontierless horizons.

But to get back to the chewing gum and cigarettes. We children didn't care much for the cigarettes, but we did like the devilishly tasty chewing gum. We rarely got a piece, though, because the grownups kept it for themselves. Our only chance was to get involved in some illicit operation, like when Chama wanted us to go pick up a letter from her friend, Wassila Bennis. Samir and I knew that those letters were actually written by

Wassila's brother, Chadli. Chadli was in love with Chama, but we were not supposed to know that. At any rate, Father and Uncle did not like there to be too much coming and going between our two houses, both because the Bennises had many sons and because Mrs Bennis was a Tunisian of Turkish descent, and therefore extremely dangerous. A practitioner of Kemal Atatürk's revolutionary ideas,[2] she drove around unveiled in her husband's black Oldsmobile, just like a French woman, and wore her hair platinum-tinted and cut like Greta Garbo's. Everyone agreed that she did not really belong in the Medina. Still, whenever Mrs Bennis went out in the old city, and she did go out often, she dressed according to tradition, in a *djellaba* and veil. Indeed, you could say that Mrs Bennis led two lives – one in the Ville Nouvelle, or European city, where she paraded about unveiled; and the other in the traditional Medina. It was this idea of a double life which excited everyone, and made Mrs Bennis a celebrity.

To live in a combination of two worlds was much more appealing than living in just one. The idea of being able to swing between two cultures, two personalities, two codes, and two languages enchanted everyone! Mother wanted me to be like Princess Aisha (the teenage daughter of our King Mohammed V who made public speeches in both Arabic and French) who wore both long caftans and short French dresses. Indeed, we children found the thought of switching codes and languages to be as

---

[2] Turkey had undergone a great political and cultural upheaval with the establishment of the Republic of Turkey in 1923 by its first president, the nationalist hero Kemal Atatürk. His government abolished numerous traditional institutions such as harems and polygamy, men's wearing of the fez, and, to a lesser extent, the wearing by women of the veil (which became optional). Aggressive economic and social reforms followed; women were granted the right to vote in 1934. Kemal Atatürk died in office in 1938.

spellbinding as the sliding open of magic doors. The women loved it too, but the men did not. They thought it was dangerous, and Father especially did not like Mrs Bennis, because he said that she made trespassing seem natural. She stepped too easily out of one culture and into another, without any regard for the *hudud*, the sacred boundary. 'And what's so wrong with that?' asked Chama. Father replied that the frontier protected cultural identity, and that if Arab women started imitating European ones by dressing provocatively, smoking cigarettes, and running around with their hair uncovered, there would be only one culture left. Ours would be dead. 'If that is so,' argued Chama, 'then why can my male cousins run around dressed like so many imitation Rudolph Valentinos and cut their hair like French soldiers, with no one screaming at them that our culture is about to disappear?' Father did not answer that question.

Father, who was a pragmatic man, was convinced that our deadliest threat came not from the Western soldiers, but from their suave salesmen peddling innocent-looking products. He therefore organized a crusade against chewing gum and Kool cigarettes. As far as he was concerned, smoking a tall, thin, white Kool cigarette was equivalent to erasing centuries of Arab culture. 'The Christians want to transform our decent Muslim households into a marketplace,' he would say. 'They want us to buy these poisonous products they make that have no real purpose, so that we turn into a whole nation of ruminating cattle. Instead of praying to Allah, people stick dirt in their mouths all day long. They're regressing to infancy, when the mouth has to be kept constantly busy.' Father's insistence on the danger of cigarettes – they were worse than the French and Spanish bullets, he said – made me feel uneasy about keeping him uninformed about the activities on the terrace. I did not want to betray his trust. He loved me very much, and expected me never to lie. But, in fact, there were hardly any cigarettes around, for it was very difficult to get them. Neither the women nor the young men had much cash, and so their purchases were rare. The buying and selling of goods in the harem was controlled by the adult males. The rest of us just consumed what was there. We did not have the privilege to choose, to decide, to buy. So buying anything, even just cigarettes, mean that illegal money was going around. That was another reason why Father tried to track down whoever was responsible for the contraband.

Since money was so scarce, to have a whole pack of cigarettes on the terrace was very unusual. Most of the time, the grownups only had one or two, and then five or six people would be smoking them. That did not really matter because it was the ritual, not the quantity, that was important. First, you stuck the cigarette in a cigarette-holder, the longer the better. Then you took the cigarette-holder between two extended fingers, closed your eyes and took a puff, with your eyes still closed. Then you opened your eyes and looked at the cigarette between your fingers as if it were some magical apparition. Next, you gave it to the person sitting beside you, who gave it to the person next to her, until the entire circle had had a puff. Oh! I almost forgot about the silence: the entire operation had to be performed without making a sound, as if pleasure had paralyzed your tongue. Sometimes, Samir, Malika, and I would imitate the grownups, using a stick instead of a cigarette, but although we copied every little gesture, we could not imitate the silence. That was the only difficult part of the ritual, as far as we were concerned.

The chewing gum and the cigarettes had come to us via the Americans who had first landed at the Casablanca Airport in November 1942. Years after they had left, the Americans kept coming up in our conversations, because everything concerning them was a mystery from beginning to end. They had appeared from out of nowhere when no one had expected them, and had surprised everyone during their short stay. Who were these strange soldiers? And why had they come? Neither Samir nor I, nor even Malika, could unravel these mysteries. All we knew for certain was this: the Americans were Christians, but they were very different from the usual ones who kept coming down from the North to give us beatings. Believe it or not, the Americans did not live in the North, but on some faraway island to the West called America, and that was why they had come by ship. Opinions varied as to how they had gotten to their island in the first place. Samir said that they were fooling around in a boat off the Spanish coast one day, when a current caught them and took them across. Malika said that they had gone there looking for gold, lost their way and decided to settle down. In any case, the Americans could not walk places like everyone else, but had to fly or go by ship whenever they got bored or wanted to visit their Christian cousins, the Spanish and the French. They could not have been very close cousins, though. The French and the Spanish were rather small and had black mustaches, while the Americans were very tall with devilish blue eyes. As Hussein Slaoui, the Casablanca folk singer, described, they scared much of the city's population when they landed, because of their combat uniforms, shoulders twice as broad as those of the French, and the fact that they started chasing women immediately. Hussein Slaoui called this song 'Al-ᶜAin az-zarga jana b-kul khir' (The Blue-Eyed Guys Brought All Kinds of Blessings), and Aunt Habiba explained that he was being sarcastic, because the Casablanca men really were quite upset. Not only did the Americans chase women whenever they spotted one from the docks, but they also gave them all kinds of poisonous gifts, such as chewing gum, handbags, scarves, cigarettes, and red lipstick.

Everyone said that the Americans had come to Morocco to

beat someone, but Samir and I did not know who. Some said they had come to beat the Allemane (Germans), those warriors who were after the French because they did not like their hair color. It seemed that the French had called on the Americans to join in the war, and help beat the Allemane. But the problem with that explanation was that there were no Allemane in Morocco! Samir, who traveled often with Uncle and Father, swore that he had seen no Allemane in the entire kingdom.

But at any rate, everyone was very happy that the Americans had not come to make war on us. Some even said that the Americans were very friendly and spent most of their time playing sports, swimming, chewing gum, and shouting 'OK' at everyone. 'OK' was their salute; it was the equivalent of our *Salam alikum* (Peace upon you). In fact, the two letters *o* and *k* stood for longer words, but the Americans had a habit of shortening their sentences so they could get back to chewing gum. It was as if we greeted one another by saying a brief *SA* instead of spelling out *Salam alikum*.

The other intriguing thing about the Americans was that they had blacks among them. There were blue-eyed Americans, and there were black Americans, and this surprised everyone. America was so far from the Sudan, the heart of Africa, and it was only in the heart of Africa that blacks were found. Mina was certain of that, and everyone else agreed with her. Allah had given all the blacks one big land with thick forests, gushing rivers and beautiful lakes, just below the desert. So where had these black Americans come from? Did Americans have slaves, like the Arabs in the past? Believe it or not, when we asked Father that question, he said yes, the Americans had had slaves, and those black Americans were definitely Mina's cousins. Their ancestors had been captured long ago, and taken in boats all the way to America to work on big plantations. Things were different now, though, Father said. Now, the Americans used

194

machines to do the work and slavery was most decidedly banned.

However, we could not figure out why, unlike the Arabs, white and black Americans did not mix and become just brown skinned, which was what usually happened when a population of whites and blacks lived together. 'Why are the American whites still so white,' asked Mina, 'and the blacks still so black? Do they not intermarry?' When finally Cousin Zin gathered enough information to answer her question, it turned out that indeed, Americans did not intermarry. Instead, they kept the races separate. Their cities were divided into two medinas, one for the blacks and one for the whites, like we had in Fez for the Muslims and the Jews. We had a good laugh about that up there on the terrace, because anyone who wanted to separate people according to their skin color in Morocco was going to run into severe difficulties. People had mixed together so much that they came in hues of honey, almond, *café au lait*, and so many, many shades of chocolate. In fact, there often were both blue-eyed and dark-skinned brothers and sisters in the same family. Mina was really stunned at the idea of separating cities according to race. 'We know that Allah separated men from women so as to control the population,' she said, 'and we know that Allah separated the religions, so that each group could conduct its own prayer, and invoke its own prophet. But what is the purpose of separating blacks from whites?' No one could answer that one question. It was one more mystery to be added to the rest.

But really, in the end, the most troubling of all the mysteries remained the question of why the Americans had landed in Casablanca in the first place. One day, I got so tired of trying to answer this question that I told Samir that maybe they had just come for a picnic. Just to visit, because they thought Casablanca was simply an island, with no inhabitants at all. Samir got upset at this and told me that if I was going to drift into silliness, he was going to quit the discussion. I begged him not to, and to mollify him, I said that I was sure there must be 'a serious political reason,' as Father would say, why the Americans had landed in Casablanca. I then suggested that we look at all the elements of the situation very carefully.

While I was saying this, I secretly was thinking that I had been having a lot of difficulties with Samir lately; he had become so serious suddenly, everything had to be political, and whenever I disagreed with him, he argued that I did not respect him. So I either had to go along with him and censor my own ideas, or else make the decision to rupture our close friendship. Of course, I never seriously considered this last option because I was afraid to face the grownups by myself. Whenever I wanted to get something, or stage a revolt, all I needed to do was whisper the idea to Samir, and he would raise hell. And all I needed to do after that, was to sit closely by, assist him when he needed a push, and cheer him when he succeeded. Take the American mystery, for example. I had thought that the idea of warriors sailing from their faraway island just to go on a picnic would amuse him, but it did not. 'You keep mixing things up,' he argued, very earnest and highly concerned about my future. 'War is war. Picnic is picnic. You always avoid looking at reality, because you are scared. What you do is dangerous, too, because you might go to sleep thinking that the warriors are in Casablanca to look at flowers and sing with birds, when they are about to come over to Fez to slit your throat. Even Malika, who is much older than I, talks this nonsense. I think it is a problem with women.' I kept very quiet at those enigmatic words because what he said sounded at the same time both bizarre and right.

The biggest problem we had with the Americans really was the one of enemies. Because if there were no Allemane in sight, why had the Americans landed in Casablanca? After many discussions, Samir came up with an explanation which made a lot of sense. He said that maybe war is like a children's game, and the Americans had landed in Casablanca to fool the Allemane, just like we hid in the olive jars to fool each other. Morocco was the Americans' olive jar. They were hiding here, and would later sneak north to attack the Allemane. I thought that Samir was very clever for thinking of this, and wished that I could travel like he did. It was his wandering around with Uncle and Father which made him so clever.

I knew that if you moved around, your mind worked faster, because you were constantly seeing new things that you had to respond to. And you certainly became more intelligent than someone stuck in a courtyard. Mother was completely convinced of this too, and said that much of the reason why men kept women in harems was to prevent them from becoming too smart. 'Running around the planet is what makes the brain race,' said Mother, 'and to put our brains to sleep is the idea behind the locks and the walls.' She added that the whole crusade against chewing gum and American cigarettes was in fact a crusade against women's rights as well. When I asked her to elaborate, she said that both smoking cigarettes and chewing gum were silly activities, but men opposed them because they gave women opportunities to make decisions on their own, decisions which were unregulated by either tradition or authority. 'So you see,' said Mother, 'a woman who chews gum is in fact making a revolutionary gesture. Not because she chews gum per se, but because gum chewing is not prescribed by the code.'

19

Mustaches and Breasts

Officially, men were not allowed on the terrace; it was the women's territory. That was largely because communication among separate houses was possible through their terraces – it was all just a simple matter of climbing and jumping. And how safe could the harems be, if men were allowed to roam from one terrace to the next? Contact between the sexes could all too easily occur.

Eye contact between my male cousins and our neighbors' daughters most certainly did occur, especially during the spring and summer, when the sunsets on the terraces were spectacular. Unmarried youth of both sexes often lingered up here, when the weather was nice, to watch as the unparalleled Fez sunsets, crazy with red and purple clouds, stretched their magic wings across the skies. Sparrows would be dancing away up there, as if seized by frenzy. Chama was always up there, along with her two older sisters, Salima and Zoubida, and three older brothers, Zin, Jawad, and Chakib. Her brothers were supposed to never set foot on our terrace, for they would be looking straight into the Bennis house, and the Bennis family had many girls, as well as boys, of marriageable age. But neither the Mernissi nor the Bennis youth ever obeyed the rules, and on summer evenings, they all flocked up to the romantic whitewashed terraces, so close to the clouds. Each family kept to its own ground, but glances and smiles crisscrossed and trespassed, and sinful lust floated all around. The most talented of the youth would sing the songs of Asmahan, Abdelwahab, or Frarid, while all the others held their breath.

One day at school, during a biology session devoted to the miraculous *insan* (the human being, Allah's most perfect creation), Lalla Tam explained to us how boys and girls became men and women capable of having babies. When we reached the age of twelve or thirteen, she said, or maybe even earlier, the boys' voices would get tougher, mustaches would appear on their faces, and suddenly, they would become men. (When Samir heard that, he drew a charcoal mustache on his upper lip with my mother's kohl, which I smuggled out for him from her very well-equipped vanity table.) As for us girls, we would develop huge busts and get *haq ach-har* (literally, the month due), which was a kind of bloody diarrhea. It did not hurt, it was all natural, and when it happened, we ought not be afraid. During *haq ach-har*, we would have to wear a *guedouar* (sanitary napkin) between our legs to keep it all discreet. When I came home from school that day, I immediately asked Mother for more details about the *guedouar*, and at first she was in shock. Then she started quizzing me about who had given me that information so soon. She was amazed to learn that it was none other but Lalla Tam, my teacher. 'We need to know about the human body, and Allah's wonderful design,' I explained to reassure her, for she seemed lost. 'A good Muslim ought to know all about science and biology, and the planets and the stars.' Then Mother got

really upset, because she realized that I was no longer a child –
not because I had changed physically, but because I had information that, according to her, children were not supposed to have.
For the first time, I had some kind of power over Mother, and it
was information which had given it to me.

That discussion was a turning point in my relationship with
Mother. She definitely knew that I was becoming independent.
She probably also realized that time was flying by, her first
daughter was growing fast, and her own beauty was not eternal.
If I was about to become a young woman, that meant that she
was growing old. 'What else did Lalla Tam tell you?' asked
Mother, looking at me as if I had come from another planet. 'Did
she say anything about babies?' Poor Mother, she just could not
believe that I, her little thing, could be stuffed so full with cosmic
information. I told her then that I knew I could bear a baby at age
twelve or thirteen, because by that age, I would have *haq ach-har*
and the breasts 'necessary to feed the little, munchy, grouchy
baby.' She was a little taken aback. 'Well,' she said at last, 'I
would have waited a year or two before talking about such
matters, but since it is part of your education . . .' I then
explained to her that she need not worry too much in any case,
because I had already known all about this for years, just from
the theater sessions, and the tales, and from listening to the
women talk. Now the knowledge was official, that was all. To
cheer her up, I joked that Samir's voice would soon sound just
like that of Fquih Naciri, the *imam* (preacher) of our local
mosque.

What I did not tell Mother, however, was that I was determined to become an irresistible *ghazala*, or a gazelle-like femme
fatale, and that I had already become heavily involved in dubious
shour, or magic practices involving astrological manipulations,
thanks to Chama's fortunate, absent-minded habit of leaving her
charm books strewn about. Chama kept dozens of these books in

her room, and since she never really hid them, I became tremendously adept at both memorizing magic formulas and copying down spell charts, complete with complicated arrays of letters and numbers, in the stressfully short interludes when she walked out of her room.

To perform terrace magic, I had to become very knowledgeable in astronomy as well. I would spend hours during sunsets scrutinizing the sky, and asking everyone nearby the stars' names in the order of their appearance. Sometimes people would gracefully volunteer the information; other times I would be abruptly silenced by 'Shut up! Can't you see that I am meditating? How can you talk when cosmic beauty is so overwhelming?'

As far as I was concerned, performing *shour* rituals such as burning small white candles during the new moon or burning outrageously decorated long candles during the full moon, or whispering secret incantations when Zahra (Venus) or Al-Mushtari (Jupiter) were overhead, was by far the most interesting crime committed on the terrace. We were all part of those operations, too, because the women needed us children to hold the candles, recite incantations, and do all sorts of special movements. The Milky Way would twinkle so close, we had the impression that it was shining just for us.

Bless Chama's soul, she used to totally forget about my young age when she became engrossed in the reading aloud of 'Talsam al-quamar' (Full Moon Talisman), which was a chapter from Imam al-Ghazali's *Kitab al-awfaq* pamphlet.[1] This chapter told

---

[1] It is inconceivable that Imam al-Ghazali, one of the giants of medieval Islamic scholarship, wrote such a book, which is, as I noted in chapter 18 (p. 187), a collection of rather comical 'do it yourself' recipes that combine elementary magic with simplistic astrology. Though good enough to impress eight-year-olds and adolescents, the work could not deceive a

how to chant garbled incantations on the special days and precise hours when the sky was in particular configurations. Not all of the literature about astrology and astronomy was considered to be of a dubious nature, either. Respectable historians such as Al-Mas‘udi wrote about the influence of the full moon on the universe, including plants and human beings, and their works were often read aloud.[2] I would listen carefully to what Al-Mas‘udi said about the moon: it made plants grow, fruits ripen, and animals fatten. It also caused women to get their *haq ach-har*.[3]

My God, I thought, if the moon can do all that, it can certainly make my hair grow longer and straighter, and speed up the development of my breasts, which was unfortunately far from happening. Malika, I noticed, had started moving her shoulders beautifully lately – she was walking like Princess Farida of Egypt before her divorce – but she could afford to do so because she had something going on. You would not call what she had breasts yet, but still, two little mini-tangerines were burgeoning under her blouse. As for me, I had nothing except a desperate hope that

scholar. But in fact, to attribute scientifically dubious treatises to the most brilliant of our philosophers, mathematicians, judges, and imams has been a strange but quite common practice in Arab literature. Abdelfetah Kilito, in his insightful *L'auteur et ses doubles: Essai sur la culture arabe classique* (Paris: Editions du Seuil, 1985), gives two reasons for this strange practice on the part of the actual authors: first, to escape vicious critique, censorship, and the caliphs' wrath; second, to continue to boost sales of the books, which have been selling briskly at the doorsteps of neighborhood mosques for centuries.

[2] Mas‘udi, *Muruj al-Dhahab* (Beirut: Dar al-Ma‘arifa, 1982), vol. 2, p. 212. (See equivalent p. 505 in vol. 2 of the French translation, *Les prairies d'or*, by Barbier de Meynard and Pavet de Courtelle [Paris: Editions CNRS, 1965].)

[3] Ibid.

things would soon start happening to me, too.

What really entranced me about the magic on the terrace was the fact that a little nothing like myself could weave spells around those wonderful astral bodies floating up there, and catch some of their glow. I became an expert on the names that Arabs gave to the moon. The new moon was called *hilal*, or crescent, and the full moon was called *qamar* or *badr*. Both *qamar* and *badr* also meant a stunningly beautiful man or woman, because it was then that the moon was at its brightest and most perfect. In between and after the *hilal* and the *qamar*, there were still other names. The thirteenth night was called *bayd*, or white, because of the translucent sky, while *sawad* was the black night when the moon was hidden behind the sun. When Chama told me that my star was Zahra (Venus), I started moving slowly about, as if made of a vaporous celestial substance. I felt I could spread silver wings any time I wanted to.

What I appreciated about astral magic, too, was the incredible range of its usage. You could increase a spell's power to influence key people such as a grandmother or a king, or simply the local grocer, who would miscalculate in your favor when you were paying for an expensive item if you planned your incantations well. But as far as I was concerned, only two things really mattered when it came to magic spells. The first was to make my teachers give me good grades, and the second was to increase my sex appeal.

I wanted of course to enchant Samir, even though the opposite seemed to be happening and our relationship was becoming more and more difficult. For one thing, like Father and Uncle, he was profoundly scornful of *shour*, and condemned it as being utter nonsense. That, of course, forced me to go underground a good part of the evening, and to disappear completely when the moon was full. I was forced, too, to use my incantations to attract imaginary Arab princes of my own age whom I did not yet know. Still, I was rather cautious. I did not want to cast my spells too far away from Fez, Rabat, or Casablanca, and even Marrakech seemed a bit too far, although Chama said that a young Moroccan lady could marry as far away as Lahore, Kuala Lampur, or even China. 'Allah made Islam's territory immense and wonderfully diverse,' she said. Much later, I discovered that the magic spells only worked if you knew your prince and could visualize him during the ritual. That meant that I was seriously handicapped, because after I had excluded Samir – as he had forcefully requested – there was no one I wanted to visualize. Most of the boys I played with at school were much shorter and younger than I, and I wanted my prince to be at least one centimeter taller and a few hours older. Still, I had knowledge of magic, and that gave me confidence.

If you wanted to make a man fall madly in love with you, you had to think about him intensely on a Friday evening at the precise moment when Zahra (Venus) appeared in the sky. All the while, too, you had to recite the following incantation:

Laf, Laf, Laf
Daf, Daf
Yabech, Dibech,
Ghálbech, Ghalbech,
Da^couj, Da^couj
Araq çadrouh,
Hah, Hah. [4]

Of course, for the incantation to have any effect at all, you were supposed to recite the magic words in a steady, melodious

[4] From *Kitab al-awfaq*, supposedly written by Imam al-Ghazali (Beirut: Al- Maktaba al-Cha'biya), p. 18.

voice, with no mistakes in pronunciation, and this was almost impossible, since the words were totally unfamiliar to us: they were not Arabic. How could they be, since the incantations were fragments of languages of the supernatural *djinnis*, kidnapped and decoded by gifted scholars who wrote them down for the benefit of mankind? My faulty pronunciation, I explained to myself as I dutifully chanted, was why my incantations did not have much effect, and no prince had yet appeared to ask for my hand. Mispronouncing the magic words was terrifyingly dangerous, too, because the *djinnis* could turn against you and scar your face or twist your leg for life if you angered them. If Samir, my protector, had been with me, he could have checked my mispronunciations and saved me from the wrath of the *djinnis*. But he remained totally indifferent to my nascent and sudden obsession to become a femme fatale.

When it came to magic, Mina agreed wholeheartedly with Samir, and although she was very tolerant of the rituals on the terrace, she still objected to them, saying that the Prophet was absolutely against them. Everyone else kept telling her that the Prophet was only against black magic, the kind that you conducted to hurt other people, but that when you burnt talismans, musk, or saffron, or recited magic spells during full moons to heighten your sex appeal, grow longer hair, become taller, or enlarge your breasts, that was all right. Allah was sensitive (*latif*) and full of tenderness and forgiveness (*rahim*) for his fragile and imperfect creatures. He was generous enough to understand such needs. Mina argued that the Prophet did not make such distinctions, and that all women doing any kind of magic would face unpleasant surprises on Judgment Day. The angels' records would lead them straight to hell.

But *shour*, or magic, did not really endanger the harem nearly as much as did the nationalists' decision to encourage women's education. The entire city was turned upside down when the religious authorities of the Qaraouiyine Mosque, including Fquih Mohammed al-Fassi and Fquih Moulay Belarbi Alaoui, supported women's rights to go to school, and with the backing of King Mohammed V, encouraged the nationalists to open up institutions of learning for girls.[5] Upon hearing the news, Mother immediately petitioned Father that I be transferred from Lalla Tam's Koran school to a 'real one,' and he responded by calling for an official family council meeting. Family council meetings were serious business, and were usually requested only when a family member needed to make an important decision or was faced with a paralyzing conflict of some kind. In the case of the transfer, the decision was too big for Father to make alone without the backing of the family. It was an enormous step to go from a traditional familiar institution, which up until then had been the only option available to little girls, to a nationalist primary school modeled on the French system, where girls learned mathematics, foreign languages, and geography, often were taught by male teachers, and played gymnastics in shorts.

So the council met. Uncle, Grandmother Lalla Mani, and all my young male cousins, who were well informed about the recent shifts in educational matters thanks to the local and foreign press, came to help Father make his decision. But you could not have a balanced family council without someone to back Mother, who had initiated the idea in the first place. Normally, this representative should have been her father, but since he lived far away on his farm, he sent a substitute in the form of Uncle

[5] A *fquih* is a Muslim religious authority, a scholarly expert in *fiqh*, or religious studies. His knowledge of theology grants him authority, and he often serves as a consultant to ministers and heads of state. However, by extension, the word *fquih* also has come to describe a teacher of any kind, regardless of the subject taught, whether at the primary, secondary, or university levels.

Tazi, my mother's brother, who lived next door. Uncle Tazi was always invited to our family councils whenever Mother was involved in any way, so as to insure equity and prevent a joint assault of the Mernissi group against her interests. So, Uncle Tazi was invited, the council took place, and Mother went out of her mind with joy when at the end of the council, my transfer had been accepted. I was not the only one affected either: all ten of my cousins were going, too. We all said a happy good-bye to Lalla Tam, and rushed on to the new school of Moulay Brahim Kettani, located a few yards from our gate.

The change was incredible, and I was elated. In Koranic school, we had had to sit cross-legged on cushions all day long, with only one break for lunch, which we brought with us from home. Discipline was ferocious – Lalla Tam would beat you with her whip whenever she did not like the way you looked, or talked, or recited the verses. The hours dragged on forever as you slowly learned and recited your lessons by heart. But in Moulay Brahim's nationalist school, everything was modern. You sat on chairs and shared a table with two other girls or boys. Someone was always interrupting and you never got bored. Not only did you jump from one subject to another – from Arabic to French, from math to geography – but you also spent a lot of time hopping from one classroom to the next. Between classes, too, you could sneak away, do acrobatics, borrow chick-pea snacks from Malika, and even ask for permission to go to the toilets, which were located at the other end of the building. That gave you a substantial ten minutes' worth of official leave, and even if you came back late, all you had to do was softly knock twice on the classroom door before entering. The two knocks on the door, before pushing it open and entering, sent me into ecstatic bliss because in our house, gates were either closed or open, and knocking would not do. Not only because of the thickness of the gigantic doors, and the impossibility of moving them, but also because a child was not allowed to open a closed door or close an open one. In addition to all this excitement, we now had two long breaks at school just to play in the courtyard, one in mid-morning and the other in mid-afternoon, and two prayer breaks. One was at midday, just before lunch, and the other was in late afternoon, when we would be led to the school mosque after having done our ritual washing at the nearby fountain.

But that was not all. On top of everything else, we now got to go home for lunch, and it was then that we Mernissi kids started wreaking havoc in the short section of the street between school and home. We would jump up and down around the little donkeys crossing our path, loaded with fresh vegetables, and sometimes the boys would even manage to climb up on the backs of the animals that were not loaded. I was so thrilled to be allowed out in the street at midday, and often managed to hug the small donkeys with their soft, moist eyes, and talk to them for a few minutes, before their master spotted me and started pushing me away. Ganging up on Mimoun, the grilled–chick-pea vendor, was another favorite activity of ours, but we always ended up in trouble because the number of portions he handed us never matched the amount of money he received in return. Then, he would accompany us to the gate, swearing by Moulay Driss, the patron saint of Fez, that he would never do business with us again, and that some of us would end up in hell, because we enjoyed eating things we had not paid for. Finally, after weeks of this, Ahmed the doorkeeper came up with an honorable solution: we all would deposit our chick-pea money with him in advance, and he would pay Mimoun at the end of each week. When one of us had exhausted our credit, we would be notified, along with Mimoun.

Modern school was so much fun that I even started getting good grades, and soon became intelligent, despite the fact that I was still helplessly slow at everything, from eating to speaking. I also found another way to be a star: I learned by heart many of the nationalist songs that we sang in school, and Father was so proud that he would ask me to recite them in front of Grandmother Lalla Mani at least once a week. At first, I sang just standing on the ground. Then, when I saw the effect my singing had, I asked permission to stand up on a stool. Next, I set my sights even higher by asking Father to pressure Mother into letting me wear my Princess Aisha dress while singing. The dress, which had a satin top and tulle all around, was a copy of the one that the Princess sometimes wore while accompanying her father, King Mohammed V. Princess Aisha often went around the country making speeches about women's liberation, and that had inspired Mother to have a copy of the dress made for me. Usually, I was allowed to wear it on special occasions only, because it was all white, and soiled easily. Mother hated when I dirtied my clothes. 'But stains are unavoidable if this poor child is to lead a normal life,' argued Father on my behalf. 'Besides, our girl is growing so fast, this dress might be totally useless by the end of the year.' Finally, to make my theatrical performance complete, I suggested to Father that he give me a little Moroccan flag, made to my size, to sing beside, but he turned down the idea immediately. 'There is a fine line between good theater and a circus,' he said. 'And art only flourishes when that separation is carefully maintained.'

But if things were going well for me, thanks to my new educators, things were going badly for Mother. With all the news about the Egyptian feminists marching in streets and becoming government ministers, the Turkish women being promoted to all kinds of official positions, and our own Princess Aisha urging women, in both Arabic and French, to take up modern ways, courtyard life had become more unbearable for her than ever. Mother cried out that her life was absurd – the world was changing, the walls and gates were not going to be here much longer, and yet, she was still a prisoner. And she could see no logic behind this. She had asked to go to literacy classes – a few schools in our own neighborhood were offering them – but her demand had been turned down by the family council. 'Schools are for little girls, not for mothers,' Lalla Mani said. 'It is not in our tradition.' 'And so what?' Mother retorted. 'Who is benefitting from a harem? What good can I do for our country, sitting here a prisoner in this courtyard? Why are we deprived of education? Who created the harem, and for what? Can anyone explain that to me?'

Most of the time, her questions flew away unanswered, like disoriented butterflies. Lalla Mani would lower her gaze and avoid eye contact, while Chama and Aunt Habiba would try to divert the conversation. Mother would remain silent for a while, and then reassure herself by talking about her children's future. 'At least my daughters will have a better life, full of opportunities,' she would say. 'They will get an education, and travel. They will discover the world, understand it, and eventually participate in transforming it. As it is, the world is most definitely rotten. For me at least. Maybe you ladies have found the secret to being happy in this courtyard.' Then she would turn to me and say, 'You *are* going to transform this world, aren't you? You are going to create a planet without walls and without frontiers, where the gatekeepers have off every day of the year.' Long silences would follow her speeches, but the beauty of her images would linger on, and float around the courtyard like perfumes, like dreams. Invisible, but so powerful.

20

The Silent Dream of Wings and Flights

One afternoon, the courtyard was, as usual, still and quiet, with everything in its place. But maybe it was even a little more still and quiet than usual. I could hear the fountain's crystal-clear music very distinctly, as if people were holding their breath, waiting for something to happen. Or maybe someone was working on creating a mirage. I knew from Chama's magic books and from discussions with her, that you could send images to your neighbor if you developed *tarkiz*, or the power of concentration, similar to the concentration needed to prepare yourself for prayers but more intense. Lalla Tam insisted that most of prayer was concentration. 'To pray is to create the void, to forget the world for a few minutes, so you can think about God. You can't think about God and your daily problems at the same time, just as you can't walk in two directions at the same time. If you do, you arrive nowhere or at least not where you wanted to go.'

Concentration was an important exercise also needed for

practical purposes, said Aunt Habiba. 'How can you talk or walk, not to mention embroider or cook, if your mind is not focused? Do you want to be like Stela Bennis?' I definitely did not want to be like Stela Bennis, one of our neighbors' daughters, who could never remember names. She kept asking everyone 'Who are you?' and could not store the answer in her little brain. As soon as you changed places, or she turned her head, you were faced with the inevitable question again: 'What is your name?' She was named Stela, which meant 'little bucket,' because all the information she received poured right out again like water. But although being drilled to concentrate was an important part of my education, I only became serious about it when Chama told me that through concentration I could send images to the persons around me. That magical idea reminded me how I had sometimes heard Chama plotting with Aunt Habiba and Mother to induce everyone in the courtyard to grow wings.

Aunt Habiba said that anyone could develop wings. It was only a matter of concentration. The wings need not be visible like the birds'; invisible ones were just as good, and the earlier you started focusing on the flight, the better. But when I begged her to be more explicit, she became impatient and warned me that some wonderful things could not be taught. 'You just keep alert, so as to capture the sizzling silk of the winged dream,' she said. But she also indicated that there were two prerequisites to growing wings: 'The first is to feel encircled and the second is to believe that you can break the circle.' After a brief, embarrassed silence, Aunt Habiba added another piece of information, all the while nervously fidgeting with her headdress, which was a sign that she was about to throw some unpleasant truth in my face. 'A third condition, as far as you are concerned, my dear, is that you stop bombarding people with questions. Observing is as good a way to learn, too. Listening with stitched lips, wakeful eyes, and quivering ears can bring more magic into your life than all the hanging around you do on that terrace, spying on Venus or peeping at the new moon!'

That conversation triggered in me both anxiety and pride at the same time. Anxiety, because apparently my clandestine initiation into magic, incantations, and charm books was no longer a secret. Pride, because whatever my secrets were, they belonged more to the domain of adults than they did to the domain of children. Magic was a more serious secret than was stealing fruits before dessert, or running away without paying all that was due to Mimoun, the chick-pea vendor. I also was proud because I understood that magic, like ice cream, came in many flavors. The weaving of fine threads between myself and the stars was one kind; focusing on strong invisible dreams and spreading out wings from within, was another, more elusive, one. No one seemed to be willing to help me visualize this second method though, and if it was described in Chama's books, I had never had enough time to read that far.

On that memorable afternoon, I had the strange sensation that someone was manipulating the growth of wings or tossing visions of flights into that seemingly quiet courtyard. But who was the magician? I stitched my lips shut, opened my ears, and looked around. The women, engrossed in their embroidery, were divided into two teams. Each one was concentrating in silence, intent on her own design. But when there was that kind of total silence in the courtyard, it meant that a wordless war was going on. And anyone who looked carefully at the embroidery projects would know what that war was all about: the eternal split between *taqlidi*, or the traditional, and *ʿasri*, or the modern. Chama and Mother, representing the modern camp, were embroidering an unfamiliar object which looked like a big bird's wing, spread in full flight. It was not their first bird of flight, but evidently, its shock value was as great as ever because the other camp, headed by Grandmother Lalla Mani and Lalla Radia, had condemned the work, as they had all the others, saying that it was totally unbecoming to its creators. They themselves were stitching a traditional design. Aunt Habiba was on their side, sharing their *mrema* (loom), but only because she could not afford to openly declare herself a revolutionary. She stitched in silence, minding her own modest business.

The modern camp, on the other hand, was not at all modest. In fact, Chama and Mother looked rather ostentatious, as they were wearing the latest copies of one of Asmahan's notorious hats, a black velvet cap with tiny pearls covering its brim. The cap had a triangular flap falling over the forehead, with the word 'Vienna' embroidered on it, and from time to time, Chama or Mother would hum the words of the infamous song, 'Layali al-unsi fi Vienna' (Nights of Pleasure in Vienna), which had inspired the cap. Lalla Mani would frown whenever they hummed because she considered the song, about decadent fun in a Western capital, to be an affront to Islam and its ethical principles. Once Samir tried to find out what was so special about Vienna, and Zin told him that it was a city where people danced to something called the waltz, all through the night. A man and a woman would hold each other very tight, and dance away, revolving around each other until they fainted with love and pleasure, just like in a possession dance. The only difference was that the women did not dance alone, they danced with men. And all this hugging and dancing took place in beautifully decorated nightclubs or even in the streets, during festivals, with city lights shimmering in the dark, as if to celebrate the lovers' embrace. Snorted Lalla Mani, 'When decent Muslim housewives start dreaming about dancing in obscene European cities, it is the end.'

Lalla Radia, Chama's mother, had been opposed to her daughter wearing the Vienna hat at first, and had accused Mother of being a bad influence on her. Relations between Lalla Radia and Mother had gotten so tense, they hardly had spoken to each other for a while. But then Chama had gone into such a stupor, and had been seized by such a severe case of *hem* (depression), that not only had Lalla Radia changed her position on the matter, but she also had gone so far as to place the Vienna hat on her daughter's head herself. Nonetheless, it still had taken some time before Chama shook off her fixed, unblinking stare.

On this particularly magical afternoon, Lalla Mani went on and on about the need to conform to *taqlid*, tradition. Anything which violated our ancestors' legacy, she said, could not be considered aesthetically valuable, and this applied to everything from food and hairstyles to laws and architecture. Innovation went hand in hand with ugliness and obscenity. 'You can be sure that your ancestors have already discovered the best ways of doing things,' she said, looking directly at Mother. 'Do you think you are more clever than the entire chain of generations that went before you and fought for the best?' To do anything new was *bidᶜa*, a criminal violation of our sacred tradition.

Mother stopped embroidering for a moment to answer Lalla Mani. 'Every day, I sacrifice myself and give in to tradition so that life can roll peacefully along in this blessed house,' she said. 'But there are some very personal things, like embroidery, which allow me to breathe, and I am not going to give those up, too. I have never enjoyed traditional embroidery, and I don't see why people can't stitch whatever they like. I don't harm anyone by creating a strange bird, instead of embroidering the same old desperately repetitive Fez design.'

The wings that Chama and Mother were stitching were those of a blue peacock, and they were embroidering them onto red silk *qamis* made to fit Chama. As soon as the *qamis* was finished, they would embroider a second one, made to fit Mother.

Women who shared the same ideas often dressed alike to show their solidarity.

Chama's peacock was inspired by Scheherazade's 'The Tale of the Birds and Beasts.' Chama loved the story, because it combined two things she adored, birds and uninhabited islands. The story began when the birds, led by the peacock, fled away from a dangerous island to a safe one:

> 'It has reached me O auspicious king,' said Scheherazade to her husband on the hundredth and forty-sixth night, 'that in times of yore and in ages long gone before, a peacock abode with his wife on the sea-shore. Now the place was infested with lions and all manner wild beasts, withal it abounded in trees and streams. So cock and hen were wont to roost by night upon one of the trees, being in fear of the beasts, and went forth by day questing for food. And they ceased not thus, to do till their fear increased on them and they searched for some place wherein to dwell other than their old dwelling-place; and in the course of their search behold, they happened on an island abounding in streams and trees. So they alighted there and ate of its fruits and drank of its waters.[1]

What thrilled Chama about this story was the fact that when the couple did not like the first island, they went looking for a better one. The idea of flying around to find something which would make you happy when you were discontented with what you had, entranced Chama, and she made Aunt Habiba repeat the beginning of the story over and over again, never seeming to have enough of it, until the rest of the audience started resenting

[1] Burton's translation, vol. 3, p. 116.

her interruptions. 'You are literate, you can read the book,' they said, 'so go and read it a hundred times if you want to, and let Aunt Habiba continue. Stop interrupting!' Everyone was so anxious to know what happened to the birds, for they identified strongly with those fragile yet adventurous creatures undertaking dangerous trips to strange islands. But Chama pleaded that reading it was not the same as listening to Aunt Habiba string the words so beautifully together.

'I want you to understand the meaning of the story, ladies,' Chama would say, looking defiantly at Lalla Mani. 'This story is not about birds. It is about us. To be alive is to move around, to search for better places, to scavenge the planet looking for more hospitable islands. I am going to marry a man with whom I can look for islands!' Aunt Habiba would then beg her not to use poor Scheherazade's tale as her own propaganda, and disunite the group again. 'Please, let us return to the birds, for God's sake,' she would say, and then continue with her story. But in fact, although Aunt Habiba referred to the women as a group, deep down there was no cohesion at all. The split between the women was unbridgeable, with the conflict over the embroidery design emblematic of much deeper, antagonistic world views.

Taqlidi (traditional) embroidery was an ostentatious and time-consuming endeavour, while *ʿasri* (modern) designs were pure fun, meant for personal enjoyment. *Taqlidi* embroidery was tedious; you had to make very tight stitches with thin thread for hours, just to cover a few inches of material. Often used for traditional bridal items, such as cushions and bed-spreads, *taqlidi* embroidery took months to finish, sometimes years. The stitches had to look identical on both sides, and the connections between the threads had to be woven in so the knots never showed on the back. Lalla Radia, who had many daughters of marriageable age, needed a lot of *taqlidi* embroidery for their trousseaus. In contrast, the birds that Chama and Mother designed did not take much time to embroider at all. Their stitches were looser, they used doubled thread, and the careless, prominent knots that showed on the backside of their cloths were to be expected. Still, the effect was just as lovely as *taqlidi* embroidery, or maybe even more so, thanks to the excitement of the unexpected designs and strange color combinations. Unlike *taqlidi* embroidery, which was present in household furnishings, modern designs were not meant to be displayed; they were limited to less conspicuous personal items, such as the *qamis*, the *sarwal*, the head scarfs, and other articles of clothing.

Rebellion in the form of modern embroidery looked terribly satisfying, I had to admit, because you could cover meters of material in just two or three days. And you could go even faster if you tripled the thread, or loosened the stitches. 'And how can you learn discipline, if your stitches are so slack and unrestrained?' Lalla Mani challenged when I said this to her. I found her remark to be quite disturbing. Everyone kept saying that a person who did not acquire discipline would be a nothing. I certainly did not want to be a nothing. So from then on, after that remark, I spent most of my time jumping from one *mrema* to the other, tasting a little freedom and relaxation in the modern camp, and following it up with some strict control in the traditional one.

Aunt Habiba did not really enjoy the repetitive and ornate *taqlidi* needlework, and Mother and Chama knew it. But they also knew that she could not express her feelings, both because she was powerless and because she did not dare disrupt the equilibrium between the two camps. Equilibrium was essential in the courtyard, everyone knew that. From time to time though, Mother and Chama would exchange quick glances and smiles with Aunt Habiba to encourage her and let her know that they sympathized with her. 'Please Aunt Habiba, let's come back to the birds!' they would plead. Telling a story, when the audience asked for one, automatically freed Aunt Habiba from her needlework duties, and I noticed that before she resumed her narration, she would fix her gaze on the small patch of blue sky framed above us, as if thanking God for all the talents he had bestowed on her. Or perhaps she needed help to revive the fragile flame within.

The new island that the peacocks found was a paradise filled with luxurious plants and gushing springs. It was also blessedly out of the reach of man, that dangerous creature who destroyed nature:

> The son of Adam circumventeth the fishes and draweth them forth of the seas; and he shooteth the birds with a pellet of clay, and trappeth the elephant with his craft. None is safe from his mischief and neither bird nor beast escapeth him.[2]

The island was safe because it was located far away in the middle of the sea, out of reach of the humans' boats and their trade routes. The peacocks' life unfolded happily and peacefully, until one day when they encountered a troubled duck, who was subject to bizarre nightmares:

> Up came to them a duck in a state of extreme terror, and stayed not faring forwards till she reached the tree whereon were perched the two peafowl, when she seemed re-assured in mind. The peacock doubted not but that she had some rare story so he asked her of her case and the cause of her concern, whereto she answered: '. . . I have dwelt all my life in this island safely and peacefully, nor have I seen any disquieting thing, till one night, as I was asleep, I sighted in my dream

---

[2] Burton's translation, vol. 3, p. 116.

the semblance of a son of Adam, who talked with me and I with him. Then I heard a voice say to me: "O thou duck, beware of the son of Adam and be not imposed on by his words nor by that he may suggest to thee; for he aboundeth in wiles and guiles; so beware with all wariness of his perfidy . . ." So I awoke, fearful and trembling, and from that hour to this my heart hath not known gladness, for dread of the son of Adam . . .'[3]

Chama always got terribly agitated when Aunt Habiba reached that part of the tale because she was extremely sensitive to the way birds were treated on the terraces and in the streets of Fez. A common sport for the young men on the terraces was to chase and hunt sparrows, using specially-made slingshots or bows and arrows borrowed for the occasion, and the young man who killed the most birds was admired and acclaimed. But Chama often screamed and cried and sobbed when her brothers Zin and Jawad amused themselves by killing sparrows. The noisy birds would invade the sky by the hundreds just before sunset, shrieking as if afraid of the night to come. The hunters would entice them to come closer by throwing olives all over the terrace floor, and then take aim and fire. Chama would stand there looking at her brothers, and ask them what kind of pleasure they could possibly get from shooting such tiny creatures. 'Even birds cannot lead a happy life in this city,' she would say, and then mumble to herself that something must be terribly wrong with a place where even harmless sparrows, just like women, were treated as dangerous predators.

To depict the peacocks' story, Chama had initially wanted to use a much deeper blue thread to embroider on the bright red

[3] Ibid.

222

silk. But in the harem, women did not go out shopping. They were not allowed to simply step out to the Qissaria, that part of the Medina where heaps of wonderful silks and velvets of all colors were piled up in the tiny shops. Instead, they had to explain what they wanted to Sidi Allal, and he would get them what they wanted.

Chama had to wait months to get the exact red silk she was looking for, and then the matching blue a few weeks later, and even then the colors were not quite right. She and Sidi Allal did not mean the same thing by 'red' and 'blue.' People, I discovered, often did not mean the same thing by the same word, even when talking about seemingly banal things like colors. No wonder then that words such as 'harem' stirred up so much wild discord and bitter dissension. It gave me much comfort to know that grownups were as confused as I was about important things.

Sidi Allal was a third cousin to Lalla Mani, and that gave him much power. He was a fine, tall man, with a thin mustache and a fantastic gift for listening, which made many of the women jealous of his wife, Lalla Zahra. He also had extremely good taste, and wore elegantly embroidered, pale beige Turkish vests made of heavy wools over his jodhpur-like *sarwal* and fine gray leather slippers. Also, since most of the merchants in the Qissaria were his friends, they selected for him the most precious turbans, brought back by pilgrims from Mecca. Sidi Allal never attended to his duties without offering his clients a drop of perfume to pacify them, and explaining to him what one wanted to buy was a very sensuous experience. Women took time between phrases to find the exact word needed to describe the satiny feel of a fabric, the subtle tone of a color, or the delicate combination of scents, if it was a perfume they were looking for.

To get Sidi Allal to visualize precisely the silks and threads needed for an embroidery project was a terribly delicate operation, and the less gifted among the women begged the more eloquent ones to describe their dreams for them. Women's wishes had to be spelled out patiently to Sidi Allal, because without his collaboration, one could not get very far. So each woman described her dream-embroidery – the kind of flowers she wanted and their colors, the hues of the buds, and sometimes whole trees with intricate branches. Others described entire islands surrounded with boats. Paralyzed by the frontier, women gave birth to whole landscapes and worlds. Sidi Allal listened with more or less interest, according to the status of the speaker.

Unfortunately, too, Sidi Allal sided with Lalla Mani when it came to the importance of tradition and *taqlidi* designs. That preference put divorced and widowed relatives like Aunt Habiba in an awkward position. They could not possibly dream of anything but classical *taqlidi* design when talking to him, and so had to rely on more powerful women like Mother and Chama to describe the silks they needed for their more innovative cravings. Aunt Habiba had to keep her birds buried deep down in her imagination. 'The main thing for the powerless is to have a dream,' she often told me while I was watching the stairs, so that she could embroider a fabulous one-winged green bird on the clandestine *mrema* she kept hidden in the darkest corner of her room. 'True, a dream alone, without the bargaining power to go with it, does not transform the world or make the walls vanish, but it does help you keep ahold of dignity.'

> *Dignity is to have a dream, a strong one, which gives you a vision, a world where you have a place, where whatever it is you have to contribute makes a difference.*
> *You are in a harem when the world does not need you.*
> *You are in a harem when what you can contribute does not make a difference.*
> *You are in a harem when what you do is useless.*
> *You are in a harem when the planet swirls around, with you buried up to your neck in scorn and neglect.*

*Only one person can change that situation and make the planet go
   around the other way, and that is you.*
*If you stand up against scorn, and dream of a different world, the
   planet's direction will be altered.*
*But what you need to avoid at all costs, is to let the scorn around you
   get inside.*
*When a woman starts thinking she is nothing, the little sparrows
   cry.*
*Who can defend them on the terrace, if no one has the vision of a
   world without slingshots?*

'Mothers should tell little girls and boys about the importance
of dreams,' Aunt Habiba said. 'They give a sense of direction. It
is not enough to reject this courtyard – you need to have a vision
of the meadows with which you want to replace it. But, how, I
asked Aunt Habiba, could you distinguish among all the wishes,
the cravings which besieged you, and find the one on which you
ought to focus, the important dream which gave you vision? She
said that little children had to be patient, the key dream would
emerge and bloom within, and then, from the intense pleasure it
gave you, you would know that it was the genuine little treasure
which would give you direction and light. She also said that I
should not worry for now, because I belonged to a long line of
women with strong dreams. 'Your Grandmother Yasmina's
dream was that she was a special creature,' Aunt Habiba said,
'and no one has ever been able to make her believe otherwise.
She changed your grandfather, and he got in her dream and
shared it with her. Your mother has wings inside, too, and your
father flies with her whenever he can. You'll be able to transform
people, I'm sure of it. I would not worry if I were you.'

That afternoon in the courtyard, which had started with such a
strange feeling of magic and winged dreams, ended with a yet
stranger but most agreeable sensation: I suddenly felt content and
secure, as if I had entered a new but safe territory. Although I had

not discovered anything special, I felt as if I had stumbled onto something important whose name I had yet to ascertain. I knew vaguely that it had to do with both dreams and reality, but what it was, I could not tell. I wondered for a few seconds whether my blissful feeling was not due to the unusually slow sunset. Most of the time, the Fez sunsets passed so rapidly that I wondered if I had only dreamt that the day was over. But the pink clouds that crossed the remote square sky above that afternoon did it at such a stunningly leisurely pace that the stars started coming out before it got dark.

I sat closer to Cousin Chama and described to her what I felt. She listened carefully and then said I was becoming mature. I felt an irresistible urge to immediately ask her what she meant by that, but refrained. I was afraid that she would forget what she was about to say and drift into complaining about how I was always harassing adults with questions. To my amazement, she kept on talking, as if to herself, as if what she was saying concerned no one but herself. 'Maturity is when you start feeling the motion of *zaman* (time) as if it is a sensuous caress.' That sentence made me feel very cheerful, because it linked together three words that the magic books kept referring to: motion, time, and caress. However, I did not say a word; I just kept listening to Chama, who was gesturing like someone about to make an important statement.

Pushing her *mrema* forward, she threw back her shoulders and caressed her Vienna hat and then, after inserting a fat cushion behind her back, started in on a monologue, Asmahan-style. That is, she fixed her eyes on an invisible horizon, and rested her chin on a menacingly fisted right hand:

Zaman *(time) is the Arab's wound.*
They feel comfortable in the past.
The past is the lure of the dead ancestors' tent.

Taqlidi *is the territory of the dead.*
The future is terrifying and sinful.
Innovation is bid^ca, *a crime!*

Carried away by her own words, Chama stood up and announced to the quiet audience that she was about to make an important declaration. Raising her white lace *qamis* with one hand, she pranced around, bowed down in front of Mother, took off her Vienna cap, and held it out rigidly before her as if it were an alien flag. Then she started in on a tirade spoken in the rhythm of pre-Islamic poetry:

What is adolescence for the Arabs?
Please, can anyone brief me?
Is adolescence a crime?
Does anyone know?
I want to live in the present.
Is that a crime?
I want to feel the sensuous caress of each fleeting second on my
    skin.
Is that a crime?
Can anyone explain why the present is less important than the
    past?
Can anyone explain why 'Layali al-Unsi' (Nights of Pleasure)
    happen only in Vienna?
Why can't we have 'Layali al-Unsi' in the Fez Medina, too?

At that, Chama's voice suddenly drifted off into that dangerous dim whisper where you could sense tears. Mother, who knew Chama's propensity to go from laughter to depression very well, sprang up immediately, bowed, and sat Chama back down on the sofa. Then, with emphatic gestures, as if she were a queen, Mother took off her own Vienna hat, saluted the compliant audience, and carried on as if it had all been planned:

Ladies and absent gentlemen,
'Layali al-Unsi' are in Vienna!
All we need to do is hire donkeys to go north.
And the fundamental question is:
How do you get a passport for a tiny homespun Fez donkey?
And how are we going to dress our diplomatic beast?
Local or foreign?
Taqlidi *or* ᶜasri?
Think deep!
But don't forget sleep!
Answer or not.
'Your opinion will be counted not.'

21

Skin Politics:
Eggs, Dates, and Other Beauty Secrets

The critical split between Cousin Samir and myself occurred when I was tiptoeing into my ninth year and Chama declared me to be officially mature. It was then that I realized that he was not ready to invest as heavily in the skin business as I was. Samir tried to convince me that beauty treatments were of secondary importance, and I tried to convince him that nothing could be expected from a person who neglected his or her skin, since it was through the skin that we felt the world. Of course, when I said that, I was expounding Aunt Habiba's skin theory, of which I had become an enthusiastic fan. But in fact, things had begun to deteriorate between Samir and me some time before. He had started calling me ᶜAssila, or Little Honey, whenever he caught me singing a song from one of Asmahan's romantic operas in a deliberately trembling voice. ᶜAssila was an insult in the Medina streets; it meant to be sticky and gluey. You called someone ᶜAssila when he or she did not look alert, and since I was already becoming known for my absent-mindedness, I begged him not to call me that. In exchange, I promised to spare him my Asmahan-styled trills. But still, things got worse. He ridiculed my interest in charm books, talisman writing, and astral incantations, and left me alone and without protection to face the dangerous *djinnis* lurking in Chama's magic books.

Finally one day, our conflict reached a crisis point, and Samir summoned an emergency meeting on the forbidden terrace, where he explained to me that if I kept dropping out for two days in a row to take part in the grownups' beauty treatments, and attended our terrace sessions with smelly, oily masks all over my face and hair, he was going to look for another games partner. Things could not go on as they were, he said; I had to choose between play and beauty, because I surely could not do both. I tried to reason with him, and repeated Aunt Habiba's skin theory, which he already knew so well. A human being was connected to the world through his or her skin, I said, and how could someone with clogged pores feel the environment or be sensitive to its vibrations? Aunt Habiba was convinced that if men wore beauty masks instead of battle masks, the world would be a much better place. Unfortunately, Samir rejected that theory as utter nonsense, and repeated his ultimatum. 'You have to choose now. I can't go on being lonely for two days at a time with no one to play with.' When he saw how distressed I was, he relented a little and said that I could have a few days to think the matter over. But I told him that there was no need for that, my decision was already made. 'Skin first! Samir,' I said, 'a woman's fate is to be beautiful, and I am going to shine like the moon.'

Yet even as I spoke, I was flooded with a scary mixed feeling of both remorse and fear, and I prayed to God that Samir would beg me to change my mind so that I would not lose face. And, lo and behold, he did. 'But Fatima,' Samir said, 'God is the only one who creates beauty. It is not by applying henna, *ghassoul* – that vulgar clay – or any of those other dirty concoctions, that

you'll transform yourself into the moon. Besides, God says that
it is unlawful to change one's physical form, so you'll be risking
hell too.' Then, Samir added that if I chose beauty, he might
have to find someone else to play with. The choice was an
agonizing one for me, but I have to confess that I also felt, deep
down, a strange feeling of triumph and pride that I had never felt
before. I came to understand it much later. The triumphant
feeling came from the fact that I realized how important a
companion I was for Samir; he could not live on that terrace
without my wonderful presence. That feeling was extraordinary
and I could not resist pushing my luck a bit farther. So, I looked
at an arbitrary spot on the horizon, a few centimeters past
Samir's ear, made my gaze as dreamy as I could, and whispered
in a barely audible voice, which I hoped reproduced Asmahan's
femme fatale tone, 'Samir, I know you can't live without me.
But I think it is time to realize that I have become a woman.'
Then, after a calculated pause, I added, 'Our paths must part.'
Like Asmahan, I did not look at Samir while speaking to see the
devastating effect of my words. I resisted that temptation and just
kept staring at that vague point on the horizon. But Samir surprised
me by retaking control. 'I don't think you are a woman yet,' he
said, 'since you are not even nine yet and you have no breasts.
There is no woman without breasts.' I did not expect that put-
down, and I was furious. I wanted to hurt him back, badly. 'Samir,'
I said, 'with or without breasts, I have decided that from now on, I
will behave like a woman, and invest the necessary time in beauty.
My skin and hair have priority over games. Good-bye, Samir. You
can start looking for another companion.'

With those fatal words, which were to bring about big changes
in my life, I proceeded down the shaky laundry poles. Samir held
them for me without a word. Once down, I held them for him,
and he slid down in silence. We stood facing each other for
awhile, and then shook hands with a great deal of solemnity, just

as we had seen Uncle and Father do in the mosque after prayers on big festival days. Then we parted in an awesome silence. I went down to the courtyard to join in the beauty treatments, and Samir stayed aloof and sulky on the deserted lower terrace.

The courtyard was a beehive of activity, with much of it centered around the fountain, where there was easy access to water for washing hands, dishes, and brushes. Basic ingredients such as eggs, honey, milk, henna, clay, and all kinds of oils were set out in big glass jars, on the marble circle surrounding the fountain. There was plenty of olive oil, of course, with the best coming from the North, less than a hundred kilometers from Fez. But of the more precious oils, such as almond oil and argan, there was much less. These came from exotic trees which needed much sun and grew only in the South, in the Marrakech and Agadir regions.

Already half the women in the courtyard looked hideous, with pastes and gluey-looking mashes covering their hair and faces. Beside them sat the team leaders, working in a solemn tranquility, since to make a mistake in the beauty treatments could cause fateful damage. One false measurement or misstep in the blends or concocting times could result in allergies and itching, or worse still, red heads turned raven black. There were the usual three beauty teams, the first concentrating on hair masks, the second on henna concoctions, and the third on skin masks and fragrances. Each team was equipped with its own *khanouns* (small charcoal fires) and low table, completely covered with an impressive array of earths and natural dyes such as dried pomegranate peel, nut bark, saffron, and all kinds of fragrant herbs and flowers, including myrtle, dried roses, and orange flowers. Many of the items were still in their blue paper, which had originally been used to wrap sugar and then recycled by the shopkeepers to wrap the expensive items. Exotic scents such as musk and amber stood stored in lovely sea-shells, sheltered in crystal containers for extra protection, and dozens of earthen bowls filled with mysterious mixtures sat waiting, begging to be transformed into magic pastes.

Some of the most magic pastes of all were those which used henna. The henna experts had to provide at least four kinds of concoctions to satisfy the courtyard taste. For those who wanted strong, flaming-red highlights, henna was diluted with a boiling juice made of pomegranate peels and a pinch of carmine. For those who desired darker tones, henna would be diluted with a warm juice made of walnut bark. For those who wanted to simply fortify their hair, mixing henna with tobacco could bring about marvels, while for those who wished to moisturize dry hair, henna would be diluted into a thin paste and kneaded together with olive, argan, or almond oil, before being massaged into the scalp. Beauty, by the way, was the only subject upon which all the women agreed. Innovation was not at all welcomed. Everyone, including Chama and Mother, relied heavily on tradition, and did nothing without first checking with Lalla Mani and Lalla Radia.

The grownups did look frightful, covered with all those fruit, vegetable, and egg masks, and dressed in the oldest and most unsightly *qamis* they could find. Then, too, since they usually wore elaborate turbans and fancy scarves, their heads now looked terrifyingly small, with deep-set eyes and brown drippings running down their cheeks and jaws. But to make yourself as ugly as possible when preparing for the *hammam* was considered a must, largely because everyone believed that the uglier you could make yourself before entering the baths, the more stunningly beautiful you would come out. Indeed, those most successful at achieving an interesting ugliness would be applauded and presented with the 'hammam repulsion mirror,' a weird ancient glass which had lost all its silver, and had the uncanny power to distort noses and reduce eyes to Satanic dots. I never played around with that glass, because it made me extremely nervous.

Our traditional *hammam* ritual involved a 'before,' a 'during,' and an 'after' phase. The phase before the *hammam* took place in the central courtyard, and that was where you made yourselves ugly by covering your face and hair with all those unbecoming mixes. The second phase took place in our neighborhood *hammam* itself, not far from our house, and that was where you undressed and stepped into a series of three cocoon-like chambers filled with steamy heat. Some women got completely undressed, others put a scarf around their hips, while the eccentrics kept their *sarwals* on, which made them look like extra-terrestrials after the fabric had gotten wet. The eccentrics who entered the *hammam* with *sarwals* on would be the target of all sorts of jokes and sarcastic remarks, such as 'Why don't you veil, too, while you're at it?'

The 'after' phase involved stepping out of the misty *hammam* into a courtyard where you could stretch out for awhile dressed only in your towels before putting on clean clothes. The courtyard of our neighborhood *hammam* had inviting wall-to-wall sofas placed on high wooden tables so you were protected from the wet floor. However, since there were not enough sofas to accommodate everyone who frequented the *hammam*, you were supposed to take up as little space as possible and not linger long. I was so happy that those sofas were there, because I always felt terribly sleepy after leaving the *hammam*. In fact, this third stage of the bathing ritual was my favorite, not only because I felt brand-new, but also because the bath attendants, under instruction from Aunt Habiba (who was in charge of *hammam* refreshments), distributed orange and almond juices, and sometimes nuts and dates too, to help you regain your energy. This 'after' phase was one of the rare times when grownups did not have to tell children to sit still, for all of us would be lying half-asleep on top of our mothers' towels and clothes. Strange hands would be pushing you here and there, sometimes lifting your legs, other times your head or hands. You heard the voices, but could not raise your fingers, so delicious was your sleep.

At a certain time of the year, a rare heavenly drink called *zeri*ᶜ*a* (literally, 'the seeds') was served at the *hammam* under the tight supervision of Aunt Habiba, so as to insure equal distribution. *Zeri*ᶜ*a* was made of melon seeds that were washed, dried, and stored in glass jars specifically made for the *hammam* drinks. (For a reason I still cannot understand, that wonderful drink was never served anywhere else but in the *hammam*.) The seeds had to be consumed quite quickly or they would spoil, which meant that *zeri*ᶜ*a* could only be tasted during the melon season, never more than a few weeks a year. The seeds were crushed and mixed with whole milk, a few drops of orange-flower water, and a pinch of cinnamon. This mixture then sat for a while, with the pulp inside. When it was served, the jug could not be disturbed too much, so the pulp would remain at the bottom and only the liquid would be poured. If you were too sleepy to drink after the *hammam* and your mother loved you very much, she would always try to pour a taste of *zeri*ᶜ*a* down your throat, so you would not miss out on that special event. Children whose mothers had been too absent-minded to do this would start screaming with frustration when they awoke and saw the empty jars. 'You drank all the *zeri*ᶜ*a*! I want *zeri*ᶜ*a*!' they would howl, but of course, they would not get any until the next year. The melon season had a cruelly abrupt end.

But leaving the *hammam* courtyard, dressed and dutifully veiled, did not mean that the beauty ritual had come to an end. There was still another step to go: perfume. That night or the next morning, the women would dress up in their most cherished caftans, sit in a quiet corner of their salons, put some musk, amber, or other fragrance onto a small charcoal fire, and let the smoke seep into their clothes and long unbraided hair. Then they would braid their hair, and put on kohl and red lipstick. We children especially loved those days because our mothers looked so beautiful then, and forgot to shout orders at us.

The magic of the *hammam* beauty treatments and ritual came not only from feeling that you had been reborn, but also from feeling that you had been the agent of that rebirth. 'Beauty is within, you just have to bring it out,' Aunt Habiba would say, posing like a queen in her room on the morning after the *hammam*. She posed for no one but herself, with her silk scarf wrapped around her head like a turban, and the few pieces of jewelry that she had salvaged from her divorce glittering around her neck and on her arms. 'But where exactly within?' I would ask. 'Is it in the heart, or the head, or where exactly?' At that, Aunt Habiba would laugh and giggle away. 'But my poor child, you needn't go that deep and complicate things! Beauty is in the skin! Take care of it, oil it, clean it, scrub it, perfume it, and put on your best clothes, even if there is no special occasion, and you'll feel like a queen. If society is hard on you, fight back by pampering your skin. Skin is political (*A-jlida siyasa*). Otherwise why would the imams order us to hide it?'

As far as Aunt Habiba was concerned, a woman's liberation had to start with skin toning and massage. 'If a woman starts mistreating her skin, she's in for all kinds of humiliations,' she would say. I did not completely understand the meaning of that last sentence, but her words inspired me to start learning all about face and hair masks. In fact, I became so good at it that Mother would send me to spy on Grandmother Lalla Mani or Lalla Radia to see what they were putting in their beauty mixtures. I had to spy because, like many other women, they shared the traditional belief that if their beauty treatments became widely known, they would lose their power. In carrying out my missions, I became so well informed that I even considered building a career in the beauty, magic, and hope business, if becoming a successful storyteller like Aunt Habiba proved to be too arduous.

One of the face masks that I liked the best was the one that Chama used to help fade freckles, pimples, and other blemishes. I had enough freckles to keep me going for a lifetime. Chama's formula, which should be used for oily skin only, went like this: First, take a fresh egg. The only way you will know for certain that it is fresh is to have a little hen as a guest on your terrace for a few weeks. But if this proves to be too difficult, pick up an egg at your nearest grocery store. If it does not look fresh enough, paint it to a white perfection. Then, wash your hands with a natural soap. This, of course, also is not always easy to find these days, but if you cannot locate anything natural, wash your hands with the most detergent-free liquid possible. Once your hands are clean, carefully break open the egg, and throw away the yolk. Now, place the white on a flat earthenware plate. Earthenware or some kind of pottery is essential; metal cannot be used. Take a good piece of clean white *shebba* (alum) which fits nicely into your palm, and rub it vigorously into the white of the egg until it becomes full of lumps. Then, put a generous layer of this very white lumpy mixture on your face. Wait for 10 minutes until it feels dry. Finally, gently wash off your face with a cloth, made of natural fiber if possible, that has been moistened with lukewarm water. Your pores should now feel fantastically clean, and your skin smooth.

Of course, such a mask did not work for Aunt Habiba, who had very dry skin. She needed a very different formula, and one that, although it cost very little, took some planning and attention to the seasons. It went like this: During the melon season, Aunt Habiba would choose one of the ripe pulpy fruits, cut a hole in it, and stuff it full with three handfuls of just-washed chick-peas. Then she would put the stuffed melon out on the terrace, and forget about it for two weeks or so, until it had dried up into a skinny little thing. Next, she would put the melon into a large mortar (nowadays, the blender is handier), and crush it with a pestle into a fine powder. She would then store this precious powder in a sunny place, carefully folded in paper inside a tin container to protect it from the humidity. Each week, she would take out a little of the powder, mix it with plain natural water (bottled water would also do), and put it on her face for an hour or so. When she washed it off with a lukewarm wet cloth, she would sigh with pleasure and say, 'My skin loves me.'

But Chama's and Aunt Habiba's facial masks were good for cleansing only. Neither gave much nourishment to the skin. So one week, they would use their cleansing masks, and the next, they would use ones known for nourishment. Yasmina's red poppy mask and Lalla Mani's dates recipe were the best. The only problem with them both was that they did not keep, and had to be used immediately. The poppy mask was also, of course, dramatically tied to the seasons. Every year, Yasmina would await the spring with great eagerness, and as soon as the wheat was around knee-high, she would go out on horseback with Tamou to hunt for the first red poppies. Poppies grew in the rich green wheat fields all around the farm, but often Tamou and Yasmina had to ride quite far, beyond the train tracks, to steal the first flowers of the season from the neighboring fields which were more exposed to the sun. Their own farm's poppies would only follow weeks later. When they found the poppies, they made a generous harvest, coming back with gigantic red bouquets. Then that night, after enlisting the help of the other co-wives, they would spread a white sheet out on a table and delicately take the flowers apart, keeping the petals and pollen, and throwing away the stems. Next, the flowers would be placed in a big crystal jar and Tamou would send someone out to the lemon trees to pick the highest fruits, those gushing with sun and ready to pour out their juices. She would squeeze the lemon juice over the flowers and leave them to soak for a few days until they had become a soft paste. Finally, when they were ready, everyone would be invited to partake in the beauty treatment. The co-wives would rush in, queuing for their turn, and for a few hours the entire farm would be filled with red-faced creatures. Only their eyes would be showing. 'When you wash off your face, your skin will glow like the poppies,' Yasmina would say, with that insolent self-confidence that magicians have.

In the Fez Medina, Mother dreamed about poppies, but most of the time she had to fall back on more accessible beauty masks. Good dates like the ones Lalla Mani used in her masks were hard to find, too, because they had to be imported from Algeria, but they were surely easier to get ahold of than the spring poppies. I have to give myself credit for discovering the date mask, because without my spying on Grandmother Lalla Mani, Mother would never have found out her secret. And Lalla Mani's skin glowed, period. Age had not made any difference at all. Lalla Mani put hardly anything on her skin most of the time, but once a week, she wore a beauty mask for a whole afternoon. No one could ever guess what the mask was made of until Mother sent me to spy, and I found out about the dates and the milk. Lalla Mani was quite disturbed when she realized that we knew about her secret mask and from then on, we children were chased out of her salon whenever she set to work on her beauty treatments.

To make her mask, Lalla Mani would place two or three very fleshy dates in a glass of whole milk, cover it, and let it sit for a few days near a sunny window. Then she would mash the mixture with a wooden spoon, apply it all over her face, and avoid going out in the sun. The mask had to dry very slowly, a detail which I could not glean from spying, and Mother, using a lot of patience, found out for herself. 'You have to sit in front of an open window,' she told me after discovering Grandmother's secret, 'or better still, under an umbrella on a terrace with a lovely view.'

22

Henna, Clay, and Men's Stares

Father hated the smell of henna, and the stink of the argan and olive oil treatments that Mother used to fortify her hair. He always looked ill-at-ease on Thursday mornings when Mother put on her horrible, previously green but now dirty gray *qamis* (an ancient gift from Lalla Mani's pilgrimage to Mecca, which had taken place before my birth), and started running around with henna on her hair and a chick-pea-and-melon mask smeared on her face from one ear to the other. Her hip-long hair, moistened with henna paste and then braided and pinned to the top of her head, looked like an impressive helmet. Mother was wholeheartedly of the school that the uglier you made yourself before *hammam*, the more beautiful you came out afterwards, and she invested an incredible amount of energy in transforming herself, so much so that my little sister would fail to recognize her through her masks and shriek whenever she approached.

Already on late Wednesday afternoons, Father would start looking gloomy. 'Douja, I love you as natural as God made you,' he would say. 'You needn't go through all this trouble to please me. I am happy with you as you are, in spite of your quick temper. I swear, with God as my witness, that I am a happy man. So, please, why don't you forget about the henna tomorrow.' But Mother's answer was always the same. 'Sidi (my lord), the woman you love is not natural at all! I have been using henna since I was three. And I need to go through this process for psychological reasons too – it makes me feel reborn. Besides, my skin and hair are silkier afterwards. You can't deny that, can you?'

So, on Thursdays, Father would sneak out of the house as early as he could. But if, by chance, he needed to come back, he would run away from Mother whenever she came near. It was a game that the courtyard loved. Occasions when men showed any terror in front of women were rare indeed. Mother would start chasing Father between the columns, and everyone would be screaming with laughter, until Lalla Mani, in her imposing headdress, appeared on her threshold. Then everything would come to a sudden stop. 'You know, Madame Tazi,' she would call out, using my mother's family name to remind her that she was a stranger in the family, 'in this respected household, husbands are not to be terrorized. Maybe at your father's farm that's how things are. But here, in the middle of this very religious city, and only a few meters away from the Qaraouiyine Mosque – one of the centers of Islam worldwide – women behave by the book. They are obedient and respectful. Outrageous behavior of the type practiced by your mother Yasmina is only good for entertaining peasants.' At that, Mother would look furiously at Father, and then disappear upstairs. She hated the harem's lack of privacy and the constant interference of his mother. 'Her behavior is unbearable and vulgar too,' Mother would say, 'especially for someone who is always lecturing about manners and respect for others.'

At the beginning of their marriage, Father had tried to keep Mother away from traditional beauty treatments by getting her to use the French beauty products which took much less time to prepare and had immediate results. Beauty products were the only area in which Father favored the modern over the traditional. After long consultations with Cousin Zin, who translated the beauty ads in the French newspapers and magazines for him, he made a long list. Then they went shopping in the Ville Nouvelle, coming back with a big bagful of beautiful packages, all wrapped in cellophane and tied with colorful silk ribbons. Father asked Zin to sit down in our salon while Mother opened the packages, in case she needed help understanding the French directions, and looked on with a great deal of interest as she carefully opened each item. It was evident that he had spent a fortune. Some packages were hair dyes, others shampoos, and then there were three kinds of creams for both the face and the hair, not to mention perfume in jewel-like bottles. Father especially disliked the musk fragrance that Mother insisted on putting on her hair, and so he eagerly helped her open the bottle of Chanel No 5, swearing that 'It has all the flowers in it that you like the best.' Mother looked at everything with a lot of curiosity, made some inquiries about their composition, and asked Zin to translate the instructions. Finally she turned to Father and asked him a question he did not expect. 'Who made these products?' He then made the fatal mistake of telling her that they had been made by scientific men in clinical laboratories. Upon hearing that, she picked up the perfume, and threw everything else away. 'If men are now going to rob me of the only things I still control – my own cosmetics – then they will be the ones who have power over my beauty. I will never allow such a thing to happen. I create my own magic, and I am not relinquishing my henna.' That settled the matter once and for all, and Father had to resign himself, along with all the other men in the courtyard, to the inconveniences of the beauty treatments.

On the night before the *hammam*, when Mother put henna in her hair, Father deserted our salon and took refuge at his mother's. But he would always come back immediately when Mother returned home, wearing Chanel No 5. She would stop by Lalla Mani's salon first to kiss her hand. That was a traditional ritual. A daughter-in-law was obliged to stop at her mother-in-law's to kiss her hand after the *hammam*. However, thanks to the nationalist revolution and all the talk about women's liberation, the ritual was dying out in most places, except for on important religious festival days. Still, since Lalla Radia continued to respect the ritual, Mother had to do so as well.

But Mother also used the hand-kissing ritual as an opportunity to joke a little. 'Dear Mother-in-law,' she would say, 'do you think your son is ready to face his wife again, or does he want to stay with mom?' Mother would be smiling as she spoke, but Lalla Mani would respond with a frown, and raise her chin. She thought that humor in general was a form of disrespect, and that when it came from Mother, in particular, it was a kind of straightforward aggression. 'You know dear,' she would inevitably retort, 'you are lucky to have married such an easygoing man as my son. Others would have cast out a wife who disobeyed them and insisted on putting henna in her hair when they begged her not to. Besides, don't forget that Allah has given men the right to have four wives. If my son ever uses his sacred right, he could go to his second wife's bed, when you drive him out with your henna stink.' Mother would listen to Grandmother calmly and serenely, until she finished her sermon. Then, without another word, she would kiss her hand and proceed towards her own salon, with Chanel No 5 trailing close behind.

The *hammam* that we went to in order to bathe and wash off our beauty treatments was all white marble walls and floors, with a lot of glass in the ceilings to keep the light flowing in.

That combination of ivory light, mist, and nude adults and children running all around made the *hammam* seem like a steamy-hot, exotic island that had somehow become adrift in the middle of the disciplined Medina. Indeed, the *hammam* would have been paradise, if it had not been for its third chamber.

The first chamber of the *hammam* was steamy, yes, but nothing exceptional, and we passed through it quickly, using it mainly as a way to get used to the misty heat. The second chamber was a delight, with just enough steam to blur the world around us into a sort of extraterrestrial place, but not enough to make breathing difficult. In that second chamber, women would get into a cleansing frenzy, sloughing off dead skin with *mhecca*, or round pieces of cork wrapped up in hand-crocheted woolen covers.

To wash out the henna and oils, the women used *ghassoul*, a miraculous clay shampoo and lotion which made your hair and skin feel incredibly smooth. 'The *ghassoul* is what transforms your skin into silk,' claimed Aunt Habiba. 'That's what makes you feel like an ancient goddess when you step out of the *hammam*.' It took many seasons, and two to three days of hard work, to make *ghassoul*, which was actually fragrant brown chips of dried clay. Once they were made, all you needed to do with the chips was to sprinkle a handful of them into rosewater, and you had a magical solution.

The making of *ghassoul* started in the spring, and the whole courtyard would get involved. First, Sidi Allal would bring in heaps of rosebuds, myrtle, and other fragrant plants from the countryside, and the women would rush to take them upstairs and spread them out on clean sheets away from the sun. Once dried, the flowers would be put away until the big *ghassoul*-making day in mid-summer, when they would be combined with clay and dried again into a thin crust – this time by the hot summer sun. No child ever wanted to miss that day because then, not only did the grownups need our assistance, but we were also allowed to knead the clay and become as dirty as we liked, with no one complaining. The perfumed clay smelled good enough to eat, and once Samir and I did try some, only to come down with stomach aches which we kept carefully secret.

As with the other beauty treatments, the making of *ghassoul* took place around the fountain. Women would bring their stools and charcoal fires, and sit near the water, so as to be able to wash their hands and pots and pans easily. First, kilos of dried roses and myrtle would be placed in separate deep pots and left to simmer slowly for a while. Then, they would be taken off the fire, and allowed to cool down. Women who were fond of a special kind of flower – like Mother, who loved lavender – would put these flowers in smaller pots to simmer. Again, as with the other beauty treatments, some women believed that all the magical effect of their *ghassoul* formula would evaporate if it became common knowledge, and so these women would disappear into dark corners on the top floors, close doors, and mix their mysterious plants and flowers in secrecy. Some women, like Aunt Habiba, dried their roses in the moonlight. Others restricted themselves to flowers of specific colors, and still others recited magic incantations over their plants to enhance their enchanting powers.

Then the kneading process would start. Aunt Habiba would give the signal by putting a few handfuls of raw clay in a wide earthenware pan like those used to knead bread. She would then pour a bowlful of myrtle or rosewater over the clay, allow it to sink in, and start kneading it until it became a smooth paste. Next, she would spread the paste over a wooden board, and call on us children to take the board to the terrace to dry.

We children loved that part, and sometimes one of us would get so excited that he forgot that the clay was still soft, and started running faster and faster, until the whole contents of the board slipped off onto his head. That was horribly embarrassing, especially because then someone would have to lead him back down to the courtyard, his eyes sealed shut with clay. This kind of incident never happened to me, however, since I was so desperately slow in everything. But *ghassoul*-making day was one of the rare occasions when that quality was appreciated.

Once we children emerged on the terrace with the wooden boards on our heads, huffing and puffing away to show how important our contribution was, Mina would take charge. Her job was to watch over the boards and monitor the drying process. At night, she would instruct us to take the boards in, so that the humidity would not affect them, and around noon the next day, when the sun was hot, she would instruct us to bring them back out again. After five days, the clay would have dried into a thin crust, and split into small pieces. Then, Mina would dump it all out onto one big clean sheet and divide it up among all the adult women. Those who had children got proportionally more, because their needs were greater.

Ghassoul was used in the second chamber of the *hammam* as a shampoo, and in the third and hottest chamber, where the most compulsive cleansing took place, as a smoothing and cleansing cream. Samir and I hated that third room, and even called it the torture chamber, because it was there that the grownups insisted on 'seriously' taking care of us children. In the first two chambers of the *hammam*, the mothers would forget about their offspring, so involved were they with their beauty treatments. But in the third chamber, just before undertaking their own purification rituals, the mothers felt guilty about neglecting us, and tried to make up for it by turning our last moments in the *hammam* into a nightmare. It was then and there that everything suddenly went wrong, and we started sliding from one misfortunate experience to the next.

First of all, the mothers filled buckets of cold and hot water directly from the fountains, and poured it over our heads before testing it properly first. And they never succeeded in getting the right temperature. The water was either scaldingly hot or ice cold, never anything in between. Officially, too, we were not even allowed to scream in the third chamber because all around us, the women were conducting their purification rituals. To purify oneself, that is, to prepare for the prayer that took place immediately after stepping out of the *hammam*, adults needed to use the purest of waters. The only way to insure that purity was to be as near to the source (in this case, the fountains) as possible. That meant that the third chamber was always crowded and you had to line up in order to fill your buckets. (Actually, the third chamber of the *hammam* was the only place where I ever saw Moroccans line up in an orderly way.) Every minute spent waiting for that fountain was simply unbearable, because of the heat.

As soon as the buckets were filled, the adults immediately started in on the purification ritual, right at the front of the line. The ritual washing was distinguished from routine washing by a silent concentration and a prescribed order in which the body parts were washed – hands, arms, face, head, and finally the feet. You were not supposed to run in front of a woman doing her ritual, which meant that we could barely move. So between that and the too-hot or too-cold water being poured over your heads, you could always hear children shrieking and howling all over the place. Some would manage to escape from their mother's grip for a moment, but since the marble floor was slippery with water and clay, and the room so crowded, they never got away for very long. Some would try to avoid going into the third chamber in the first place, but in that case, which was often what happened to me, they would just be picked up off their feet and forced in, despite their shrill screams.

Those were the few terrible moments that practically erased the whole delightful effect of the *hammam* session, nearly wiping out in a single stroke the long string of wonderful hours spent concealing Aunt Habiba's precious Senegalese ivory comb, only to magically produce it again when she started frantically searching for it; stealing a few of Chama's oranges that she kept in a cold bucket of water; watching the fat women with huge breasts, the skinny ones with protruding behinds, or the tiny mothers with giant teenage daughters; and, most of all, comforting the grownups when they fell down on the slippery clay- and henna-coated floors.

I discovered, at one point, a way to speed up the process in the torture chamber and force mother to rush me to the door. I faked fainting, a talent at which I had already become rather skillful, to keep people from bothering me. Fainting when the other children imitated the *djinnis* as we rushed down the stairs late at night, would often result in the child who had frightened me dragging me down to the courtyard or at least alerting Mother. That, in turn, would result in Mother raising hell, and going to complain to the child's mother on my behalf. But performing my strategic fainting in the *hammam*, when I was dragged to the third chamber, was more rewarding because I had an audience. First, I would grip Mother's hand to make sure she was looking my way. Then I would close my eyes, hold my breath, and start sliding down towards the wet marble floor. Mother would beg for help. 'For God's sake, help me get her out of here! This child is having heart failure again.' I told my trick to Samir, and he tried it too, but he was caught smiling when his mother started howling for help. She reported this to Uncle ⁽Ali, and Samir was publicly chided the next Friday, just before the prayer, for fooling his own mother, 'the most sacred creature walking on two feet on God's vast planet.' Samir then had to ask her pardon, kiss Lalla Mani's hand, and ask her to pray for him. To get to paradise, a Muslim had to pass under his mother's feet (*al-janatu tahta aqdami l-ummahat*), and Samir's prospects at that moment looked rather dim.

Then came the day that Samir was thrown out of the *hammam* because a woman noticed that he had 'a man's stare'. That event made me realize that we were both somehow drifting into a new era, maybe into adulthood, even though we still looked terribly small and helpless compared to the giant-sized grownups around us.

The incident occurred one day in the second chamber when a woman suddenly started shouting and pointing at Samir. 'To whom does this boy belong?' she cried, 'He is not a child anymore.' Chama rushed up to her and told her that Samir was just nine, but the woman was adamant. 'He might be four, but I am telling you, he looked at my breast just like my husband does.' All the women who were sitting around, washing the henna out of their hair, stopped what they were doing to listen to the exchange, and they all started laughing when the woman went on to say that Samir 'had a very erotic stare.' Then Chama got nasty: 'Maybe he looked at you like that because you have a strange breast. Or maybe, you're getting an erotic kick out of this child. If so, you're going to be in for some serious frustration.' At that, everyone started laughing uproariously, and Samir, standing there in the middle of all those naked ladies, suddenly realized that he unquestionably had some kind of unusual power. He pounded his skinny chest and shouted out with aplomb his now-historic retort which became a sort of witticism in the Mernissi household: 'You are not my type. I like tall women.' This put Chama in an awkward position. She could no longer keep defending her surprisingly precocious brother, especially since she herself could not refrain from laughing along with the crowd. Their laughter reverberated around the room. But that comic incident signaled, without Samir and I realizing it, the end of childhood, when the difference between the sexes did not matter. After that, Samir was less and less tolerated in the woman's *hammam*, as his 'erotic stare' began disturbing more and more women. Each time it happened, Samir would be taken back home as a triumphant male, and his manly behavior commented on and joked about in the courtyard for days. Finally, though, news of the incidents reached Uncle ᶜAli, who decided that his son should stop going to the women's *hammam* and join the men's.

I was very sad to go to the *hammam* without Samir, especially since we could no longer play the games we had usually played during the three hours we spent there. Samir made equally sad reports on his experiences in the men's *hammam*. 'The men don't eat there, you know,' he said. 'No almonds, no drinks, and they don't talk or laugh either. They just clean themselves.' I told him that if he could just avoid looking at the women the way he did, maybe he could still convince his mother to let him join us again. But to my great amazement, he said that that was no longer possible and that we needed to think about the future. 'You know,' he said, 'I am a man, although it does not show yet, and men and women have to hide their bodies from each other. They need to separate.' That sounded profound, and I was very impressed, although not convinced. Samir then remarked that in the men's *hammam* they did not use henna and face masks. 'Men don't need beauty preparations,' he said.

That remark brought me back to the old discussion we had had on the terrace, and I felt that it was an attack on me. I had been the first to jeopardize our friendship, by insisting on my need to get involved in the beauty treatments, so I started to defend my position. 'Aunt Habiba says that skin is important,' I began, but Samir interrupted me. 'I think that men have a different skin,' he said. I just stared at him. There was nothing I could say because I realized that for the first time in our children's games, all that Samir had said was right, and that whatever I said did not matter that much. Suddenly, it all seemed so strange and complicated, and beyond my grasp. I could feel that I was crossing a frontier, stepping over a threshold, but I could not figure out what kind of new space I was stepping into.

Suddenly I felt sad for no reason, and I went up to Mina on the terrace and sat by her side. She stroked my hair. 'Why are we so quiet today?' she asked. I told her about my conversation with Samir, and also about what had happened in the *hammam*. She listened with her back to the western wall, her yellow headdress as elegant as ever, and when I had finished, she told me that life was going to be tougher from now on for both me and Samir. 'Childhood is when the difference does not matter,' she said. 'From now on, you won't be able to escape it. You'll be ruled by the difference. The world is going to turn ruthless.'

'But why?' I asked her, 'and why can't we escape the rule of the difference? Why can't men and women keep on playing together even when they are older? Why the separation?' Mina replied not by answering my questions but by saying that both men and women live miserable lives because of the separation. Separation creates an enormous gap in understanding. 'Men do not understand women,' she said, 'and women do not understand men, and it all starts when little girls are separated from little boys in the *hammam*. Then a cosmic frontier splits the planet in two halves. The frontier indicates the line of power because wherever there is a frontier, there are two kinds of creatures walking on Allah's earth, the powerful on one side, and the powerless on the other.'

I asked Mina how would I know on which side I stood. Her answer was quick, short, and very clear: 'If you can't get out, you are on the powerless side.'